POSITIVE POSSIBILITIES

My Game Plan for Success

An Autobiography

MATTHEW JENKINS, DVM

ISBN 978-1-64003-267-5 (Paperback)
ISBN 978-1-64003-268-2 (Hardcover)
ISBN 978-1-64003-269-9 (Digital)

Covenant Books, Inc.
11661 Hwy 707
Murrells Inlet, SC 29576
www.covenantbooks.com

Dr. Matthew and Mrs. Roberta Jenkins

To my outstanding parents, John Wesley Jenkins and Amelia T. Jenkins, who created a loving family environment with great moral ethics, high expectations, and fairness. Those values encouraged their children to become harmonious and productive members of society. We were taught to treat every person the way we wanted to be treated. I am privileged to have been exposed to this wholesome family training.

To my loving wife and business partner of over fifty years, Roberta Jones-Jenkins. She has been there for me through the best of times and the most challenging of times. Although a beautiful woman on the outside, Roberta is even more beautiful inside.

To my children and grandchildren, to what I've learned about life and the values I used to reach my goals. In my book, I share with you how I created my life. "You cannot know where you are going until you know where you came from." I am who you came from.

It is my hope that one day you will understand the sacrifice and joy required to live a fulfilling life. I hope this book will enhance your ability to study, work hard and set specific goals, and develop a game plan for accomplishing those goals.

Though you will face many challenges in life, always look at each obstacle as an opportunity to improve your circumstances. Always seek out the *positive possibilities* in all that you do. Most of the time, they are right in front of you.

To my daughter, Sabrae Derby, a modern businesswoman: you are my love, my ballerina.

To my son-in-law, Brian Derby: you gave us two precious grandchildren, Makarios and Amaris, who fill us with love and hope.

To Derryl Jenkins, my son by choice: I will always remember your smile, your sense of humor, and your love of music. I cherish the times we spend with your two wonderful children, Zowey and Olivia, who bring joy to our lives.

To my son, Dexter Jenkins: born with an adventurous spirit and love of travel, I admire your perseverance and stamina in the face of life's challenges.

To Della Jenkins, my daughter-in-law and caring mother of my beloved grandchildren, Bianca and Dominic: it has been my pleasure to watch them grow and achieve in academics and sports.

To all my grandchildren, you are a source of hope for new generations. I am doing my best to pass on to you love, peace, and a giving spirit to make the world a better place.

ACKNOWLEDGMENTS

This book could not have been written without the constant encouragement of those who heard me speak at various colleges and universities over the last thirty years. I kept hearing how valuable my speeches were to students, teachers, and ordinary people, and it was those people who kept reminding me to write the book. And ultimately, I did. Now I hope it is helpful to young people everywhere and to those who contributed to my story.

My dear sister, Connie, and my brothers, Levaughn and Samuel; thank you for providing me with much of the family history that began before I was born.

Tyler Reeb, PhD, Claremont Graduate University; thank you for your editorial and research assistance.

Dr. Mark Pedretti, director of the Writing Center at Claremont Graduate University; thank you for your outstanding advice and review.

Martha Tucker, Author and Publisher and my longtime friend; thank you for your assistance and advice.

John Wesley Jenkins

CONTENTS

PROLOGUE

John Wesley Jenkins: A Man
I Never Really Knew

I want to set the record straight and acknowledge and honor the man who started this story long before I was born. I recall something my family told me he often said and lived by: "Better to die right than live wrong."

John Wesley Jenkins was beaten nearly to death in Mississippi in 1890 for warning black farmers in the area that the Ku Klux Klan was plotting to take their farms or burn their crops.

After the Emancipation Proclamation, the Jenkins' family had acquired 160 acres in Shuqualak, Mississippi. My father's father, Hilliard, worked that farm with his older brothers: Willis, Alford, and Stephen. Although their families owned the land, they still needed sharecropper credit from larger plantation owners to purchase equipment and seed to plant and harvest their crops. Any sharecropper who owned the land was fortunate, but most rented the land.

Sharecroppers wanted to own their land, equipment, fertilizer, and seed in order to be free of ties to the larger plantation owners. They wanted to own their resources to reap full profit from their sales. But there was also a much deeper reason. Most of the large plantation owners who issued sharecropper contracts had been slave owners just a few years before. Many of them had raped and killed slaves.

Those plantation owners colluded with corrupt law enforcement and financial agencies to trap black farmers into signing unfair sharecropping agreements that reduced them to de facto slaves. Because of this, it's easy to see why my father's family wanted to save enough money to free themselves from any association whatsoever with white plantation owners.

I don't know how it happened, but somehow, while my grandfather and granduncles were working their farm, my father—still a boy—started working as a "house" black for a wealthy white family who owned a large plantation near my father's family farm.

He ran the vast household and his many jobs including everything from pushing oversized mops across the massive floors to shaving the owner with a straight blade razor. While carrying out his duties, my father quietly listened and absorbed all the knowledge he could from the "big house." He learned all about the owner's farming practices, how they dressed and prepared for important meetings, and even how they negotiated and reasoned during business dealings.

In short, he extracted every piece of information that would ultimately be useful for his survival. Had my father been a "field" black, his living and working conditions would have been far worse, and he would never have been exposed to that kind of information.

Surrounded by injustice, it's no mystery why my father ran away when he was fifteen. But even though he was quickly captured, beaten, and reinstalled at the plantation to do house work, his spirit remained unbroken.

You may wonder how it was possible for my father to be treated that way in the aftermath of the Emancipation Proclamation and the Thirteenth Amendment to the Constitution. It's simple, really. While the law had changed, many minds had not. Acts of hate and corruption remained the norm, and soon, the Jim Crow era was ushered into the Deep South.

With Jim Crow came new forms of oppression, driven by greed and entrenched racism. Segregation, voter suppression, vagrancy laws, and sharecropper collusion deterred democracy and ensnared working blacks into unfair contracts that turned their civil rights back to slavery in all but name.

By night, the KKK used lynchings and cross burnings to terrorize black Americans and break their spirit. What's important to understand about my father is this: although he was an eternal optimist, he refused to take the easy way out if it meant doing wrong in the process. John Wesley Jenkins never "went along to get along." That's why he didn't sit idly by when he overheard white plantation owners discussing plans to burn the buildings and ruin the crops of black farmers in the area.

In the face of almost certain death, my father notified his kin and other black farmers about the intended sabotage. Thanks to his warnings, the black farms were spared. The bad news was that word got back to the white plantation owners that my father had been the one who warned the black farmers of their plans. So they beat him again, even more viciously than before.

Though my father was greatly outnumbered, he fought to stay alive, bloody but unbowed.

His attackers dumped my badly beaten father onto a train heading to Pensacola, Florida. The conductor was told to discard the body before the train reached Mobile, Alabama. When a new conductor came aboard just outside the city limits, he noticed my father, bloody and unconscious. I'm sure he assumed my father was dead or dying, so he dumped him alongside the railroad tracks and kept moving toward Florida.

My father lay unconscious for hours beside the tracks, completely cut off from his family and the life he knew. Finally, a man on horseback saw him and promptly rode off and quickly returned with supplies to care for his wounds, which were so critical my father couldn't easily be moved. The Good Samaritan called on four trusted neighbors to help carry him to safety and mend his body so the town's only doctor wouldn't report a bloody black man to the local sheriff.

One thing I've found through all my travels is that there are good souls to be found everywhere. Caring brings people together. We never knew the name of that Good Samaritan or anything of his family, only that he'd saved my father's life and then disappeared. My father knew only that a Greek immigrant had found him and tended his wounds. That act of compassion not only saved my father's life but also began a legacy for all ten of his children to follow, including me, Matthew Jenkins.

Older family members recalled that every winter, my father would call on my older sister, Connie, to rub the deep scars etched on his back from those beatings. Cold days meant that the pain had returned from the old beatings. As Connie soothed his scarred back, my father would remind her, "Never hate, Connie. Hate kills."

One gift my father passed to all his children was never to harbor anger or bitterness in our hearts, no matter what. Even on his death-bed, he encouraged us not to harbor anger against white people or anyone else who wronged us. "Never let your mind be clouded with hate," he said.

That's how he was able to separate himself from the hateful acts of the plantation owners. I still wonder if I am half the man my father was.

◄─◄❖►─►

The deeds of that Good Samaritan marked the first of many fruit-ful relationships my father established with people from different communities and cultures in Baldwin County. Sixteen years after my father's life was saved by that Greek farmer, another Greek immigrant and humanitarian by the name of Jason Malbis purchased 120 acres in Daphne, Alabama. From that humble beginning in 1906, Malbis established a Greek colony that became Malbis Plantation, Inc.

Beginning with my father's dealings with Jason Malbis and other members of the colony, my family enjoyed a rich and mutually beneficial relationship with that vibrant Greek community. Around the same time, an Italian immigrant named Angelo Arthur Corte bought his first forty acres and began a long history of Italians farm-ing in Baldwin County, Alabama.

In the years ahead, my father would purchase his first forty acres for farming and related businesses, and our family would maintain lasting relationships with the Cortes, the Malbis, and many other good people in Baldwin County.

It's important to note that the best of Baldwin County in Alabama embodied the best values of this country. If you reach down and grab a handful of dirt from the ground where I was raised, one thing is immediately apparent—that rich black soil was capable of feeding us all.

Rich soil contains the nutrients that produce fine harvests, just as a child nurtured by wholesome values has the tools for a productive life.

The soil in Baldwin County was rich and so were its people in many ways. In the revolutionary parlance of our nation's Declaration of Independence, Baldwin County was a place where many blacks and immigrants could access their right to "Life, Liberty and the pursuit of Happiness."

Baldwin County had its share of problems, but unlike most racist communities in the Deep South, Baldwin County bore witness to many beneficial interactions between its black, white, and immigrant communities.

How would I ever measure up to my father's greatness in helping to shape a place like Baldwin County, Alabama?

FROM THE CORE OF ALL THAT I AM

Fathers are very important in shaping the lives of their children. I often wonder why any father would run off and leave his child, especially in the black community, where the need for a strong male figure is especially vital to the child's positive development.

Although my father died when I was two years old, all my life, family, neighbors, and relatives told me that I was more like my dad than any of his children. Even though he was not physically present, the stories they told me about his character, drive, and determination, as well as the respect he earned in the community, guided me to be the very best person I could be.

I have always worked hard to live my life in a way that brought honor to his memory.

The image I held of my father is what led me into manhood. In my teens, I cultivated his strong character traits, instilled in me by my family and those who knew him. In my more mature years, I traveled the country speaking at colleges and universities about *Positive Possibilities*—how I achieved success in business with my veterinary practice and real-estate development and in my family life by teaching my children exemplary values. There is not much difference between raising your children right and providing excellent customer service. They both require honesty, integrity, and keen observation. Watching your children closely will enable you to discover opportunities to teach them, and by observing your customers closely, you will spot opportunities to satisfy their needs.

Success in business and success in the home are not mutually exclusive.

Whenever I gave a speech, people would approach me afterward and encourage me to tell the world my story. For thirty years, I heard the same mantra: "You should write a book about setting goals and the steps to reach them."

Yet they didn't know the sacrifices I had made to stay on track or the will and fortitude required to focus on my goals. Most people I know resist sacrifices. They look for the easy way. As I was building my veterinary practice and developing a vast real-estate portfolio, I was also working on the Matthew and Roberta Jenkins Family Foundation to help students. But despite all that, I still wondered if my life was all it could be.

In 2010, I started thinking seriously about the value I brought to society, and by 2013, I began recording my dreams, sacrifices, goals, and successes. I wanted to record the myriad of challenges I had overcome. I believed those recordings could help anyone develop the knowledge and stamina that had allowed me to live a productive life. This project would also help me discover what would my life say about me in the end.

If I could share positive ideas with a few people at a time, perhaps, I could also reach thousands. Perhaps by doing this, I could even, in my own small way, make the world a better place to live.

Some years later, I took another big step—writing my thoughts, methods, formula, tasks, and decisions to bring value to others. I am proud to have finished this book and hope that those who read it find that it adds value to their lives.

"Every person has a life worth living; he or she only needs to take hold of that life and direct it to fulfill a specific goal using my game plan, which is clear and honest."

CHAPTER 1

Desperate Phone Call

A recurring back injury brought the idea of retirement into focus as clear as the soothing ninety-degree view of the Pacific Ocean outside my living room window. From a distance, the ocean may have looked quite peaceful, but beneath the surface was a torrent of non-stop activity. And I imagined thousands of white brain cells swirling around my head with a multitude of questions and answers about my retirement.

It was around two-thirty that sunny California afternoon, a time by which I ordinarily would have pulled off three major business meetings, possibly followed by a swim. That day, however, I felt like basking in my pending retirement. For a black man in America, the scene of the ocean outside my window felt like success and was deserving of reflection.

Life was good. If 2013 had been any better, I couldn't have imagined how. Over fifty years before, I had set my goals. And for fifty years, I followed my game plan. I had achieved what I set out to do and became a success. I had earned my retirement, and now it was my time to live!

As I sipped from a frosty glass of lemonade, gazing at the endless ocean, the phone rang.

It was Charles Williams, chairman of Tuskegee University Board of Trustees.

"How's everything at Tuskegee, Chuck?"

"Oh, the usual suspects are still kicking up trouble," he replied.

"Seems like par for the course at most colleges these days," I said.

There was a slight pause, so I waited for him to continue. I had the feeling this was more than a cordial call from an old friend.

"This time, it's bad, Matt," he added.

"Tell me something new," I said.

"No, no. It's worse now."

I felt that something was about to come out of his mouth that I didn't want to hear.

"You can always depend on me," I said, although I must confess that I was anxious to hang up and continue with pleasant thoughts of retirement.

"How would you like to come down here and help straighten things out?"

"How do you mean?" I asked.

"I'd like you to serve as interim president of Tuskegee for a year."

It was such an unexpected request that I actually laughed out loud. I didn't know what to make of his call.

"What you laughing about, Matt? We've got a serious problem!"

"Whatever gave you the idea I could solve it?" I asked.

"Your foundation's been good to Tuskegee over the last thirty-five years, Matt. And frankly, I didn't know who else to call. It's too fine a university to allow it to crumble."

"Crumble?"

My mind went into a tailspin. That tumultuous activity beneath the surface of the Pacific had nothing on my brain cells now!

I just had knee replacement surgery and was on the verge of a very pleasant retirement.

"Chuck, I'm a businessman. I'm all about crunching numbers and real estate."

"Give yourself a little time to think about it, Matt," Williams said. "This is the place that educated you and half of your family. It was once one of the finest black universities in the nation."

"I was planning to kick back and cool my heels," I answered. "Retire."

"Tuskegee might die without you, Matt."

He really knew how to turn the screws.

"Man, I'm not the right person for that," I said and quickly ended our conversation.

As soon as I hung up, the phone rang again. When I heard Chuck's voice, I was sorry I answered. *I didn't need the money, I didn't need the headaches, and I especially didn't need the work. I was going to retire!*

"Matt," he started.

"Your offer is flattering, Chuck, but it's just the wrong time for me."

"Don't say no yet," he insisted. I could hear him tapping anxiously on his phone, and somehow, his obvious desperation was tapping into the love I had always had for Tuskegee.

My mother studied there, taught by Dr. George Washington Carver. Six of my brothers and sisters attended there. Over thirty years ago, I'd served on the Tuskegee University Board of Trustees. As much as I didn't want to hear about the school's problems, the chairman's plea touched a special place in my heart.

"We've got to have someone with good managerial, organizational, and business skills. That's who we need right now."

"If I should decide to help, when would you need me there?"

"How about tomorrow?" he chuckled and then turned serious again. "Next week would be fine."

"Next week?" I laughed. "Tell you what. I'll discuss this with Roberta and get back to you."

Now the most persistent man on earth couldn't argue with another man's wife, so he finally let me off the phone to think things over, and my mind was racing. The freedom to enjoy golf, swimming, cruises, and traveling would be seriously curtailed.

My mind began to wander on some of my experiences of travel. Many years before, my family and I were arriving home from a vacation to the Caribbean. At the Miami airport, who did we see but Muhammad Ali!

Of course, we had to speak to the man. It wasn't every day you ran into perhaps the greatest boxer who ever lived, and that situation had to be dealt with.

And that was how we found ourselves in a conversation with the great Muhammad Ali, and as usual, he was boasting about just how great he was. Feeling relaxed and a little playful, I said, "Muhammad, I'm bigger than you, I'm stronger than you, and if you keep running your mouth, I might just decide to climb in the ring with you."

He was six-three, and I was an inch taller, although the rest was probably a little boasting of my own.

His eyes got wide, and he huffed and puffed and answered in that silky smooth voice, "Man, I'll blow you away before you even raise your arm."

He made a fist like he was winding up to throw a punch my way but instead curled his arm and showed off his bicep, putting on a show to the delight of the gathering crowd. My daughter Sabrae, who was seven years old at the time, reached up and gave that big old muscle of his a little punch of her own, and we all busted out laughing.

It was quite an experience.

Roberta, Sabrae, and I exchanged goodbyes with the heavy-weight champion of the world and caught a plane to Los Angeles.

I tell that story because I had planned, worked hard, and earned my dream life. That phone call from Tuskegee was still buzzing in my ears.

CHAPTER 2

❦

Decision Time

Life loomed larger by mid-2013, and I felt on top of the world. The Matthew and Roberta Jenkins Family Foundation had given many students an opportunity to attend college and start shaping a better life. Our aim was to provide educational opportunities for high school and college students and to help them improve their station in life and become productive members of society. My discipline in veterinary medicine, real estate, and other enterprises had helped me to accomplish my goal.

My son Dexter had traveled internationally for several years, spending his last two years of college in Argentina and Spain. After graduating, he worked for a company that specialized in worldwide logistics and was showing interest in taking over the family business and all that we had acquired.

I think every man wants his son to follow in his footsteps. There's nothing more satisfying than to see your son stepping up to assure the continuity, growth, and success of your life's work.

My son had gotten married and settled down, and Roberta and I were very proud of the great job he did managing our real-estate portfolio.

My daughter Sabrae was married with two sons, living in Clinton, Maryland. She still works as a board member for the Jenkins Family Foundation, and she and her husband Brian own a management-consulting firm that does business with federal, state, and local agencies. Our son Derryl in Atlanta has dreams of a music career. His young daughter and son are very much a part of our family even though they live in Minnesota and Atlanta.

That peaceful time was like the quiet before the storm. As life took on the shape of my dreams, I could feel the atoms of the universe forcing a strong wind of change. The phone call from Tuskegee University was disruptive, but also an incredible honor, given the school's historic stature. It was also a total surprise and a very big decision to make. The minute I hung up, Roberta walked into the living room carrying the mail.

"Guess who that was?" I asked, but before she could answer, I blurted out, "Chuck Williams. He wants me to come to Tuskegee and act as interim president."

"When?"

"The president resigned. Chuck thinks I need to go down there right away." I patted the seat beside me. "Have some lemonade with me."

"How long?" Roberta insisted, not yet taking the bait.

"Not more than a year," I said. Thoughts tore through my mind—leaving California, living in Alabama, canceling plans to join family and friends on a trip to Dubai, recovering from my knee surgery, enjoying my well-deserved retirement.

Going to Tuskegee would be a real mountain climb.

"What are you thinking?" she asked.

"I'm tired," I said. "I was looking forward to doing want I want."

Roberta studied me for a second and then sat on the sofa next to me.

"Look at it like this, Matt. Tuskegee has given us a lot. Given a lot to your family. This isn't something we would have planned, but we owe a lot to Mother Tuskegee."

I nodded. "Let's think of someone who can do this job until they find a new president."

"I don't think that call had anything to do with hiring someone else. Chuck called because he knew he could trust you to get the job done."

I shook my head.

"Tuskegee opened our eyes to a bigger world," she reminded me. "You'd be giving back."

"Interim president is more than a donation."

"You already served on the board," she added. "You're honest and hardworking, and they know that. They also know you won't blow up the works while searching for a president."

We bantered back and forth with the pros and cons of leaving our comfortable home and moving to Alabama for a year. We were in Tuskegee often but never more than four or five days at a time. The job would mean being on stage a lot of the time and, to a certain extent, giving up control over our lives. It was asking a lot.

"I just don't want to—"

"Helping Tuskegee could become the most rewarding part of your retirement," Roberta said, clearly warming to the challenge. "You'd be helping a deserving institution back to its former glory."

She reminded me of the deep love and admiration I held for Tuskegee, ignited by my mother long ago. Usually, we would have had opposite reactions to the Tuskegee phone call. I would have been the aggressor, and she would have been more reticent and careful in making up her mind. Her reaction touched me.

"Let's leave this weekend," I said.

I will never forget that exact moment—my acceptance of the supreme sacrifice, without pay and without regret.

Roberta smiled and stood up. "I'll start packing."

CHAPTER 3

Starting from Scratch

Roberta enjoyed our first trip to Russia, not for its beauty, but to experience the great disparity between our countries. I had worked hard for the means to travel with Roberta by land, sea, and air, and we loved it, but that love would remain unrequited. For the next year, we would be solving problems at Tuskegee University.

While in the air force, I was stationed for a time in Greenland, which is close to Russia. I took care of the dogs that guarded our ballistic missile silos deep underground, the weapons that protected the United States. I never thought about coming in direct contact with the Soviet Union, but when tensions thawed and scientific interactions were allowed, our veterinary group received clearance to visit Russian veterinary schools and facilities.

Roberta and I were the only blacks in our group, and at the airport, security allowed everyone right through, except me. They called me out of line and escorted me to a private room, questioning me about countries I had visited.

Although they let me continue, someone trailed my group most of the time. It seemed like whenever I turned around, the same two men were following me.

To my surprise, most of the Soviet professionals were women. I was not surprised, however, to find their facilities greatly inferior to ours. And both Roberta and I agreed that of all the countries we had visited, Russian food was the worst we had ever tasted. The service wasn't much better than the food. If you asked for something, the waiter would nod and leave but never return. Customer service seemed completely foreign to Soviet culture.

On the plane ride home, I sat across the aisle from Susan Eisenhower, the granddaughter of Dwight Eisenhower, who worked for her grandfather's foundation. I laughed when she shared stories of how people reacted when they connected her name to the former president.

She mentioned a rather serious back problem, and being acquainted with medicine, along with my own back and knee problems, I gave her some advice on the subject. And because we were both readers and dabbled in geopolitical issues, we had a wonderful conversation. It was good to meet such a kind and sociable lady.

My mind drifted to my past. Maybe I didn't want to confront the changes that would take place in my life over the course of a year, even with Roberta's immediate and complete encouragement.

The answer for me could be found in 1921.

There was a major fire in the basement of the Commerce Building in Washington, DC, destroying a large volume of US census records, including twenty years' worth of my father's information from 1880 to 1900. But the family assembled enough records to track my father's journey—the life of John Wesley Jenkins.

What might he have done? I wondered.

My father was born in 1874 in Noxubee County, Mississippi. His parents, Hilliard and Mariah Jenkins, were born into slavery, the property of William Jenkins, a prominent slaveholder. William Jenkins enjoyed a high standard of living due to slave labor. I imagined he was none too happy about losing his slaves after Abraham Lincoln signed the Emancipation Proclamation. But the slaveholder mentality morphed into the toxic practice of Jim Crow in the Deep South.

My ancestors, slaves who lived in Mississippi during that era, passed down the story that even on the hottest days, slave masters would let the horses drink first.

Such degradation showed how great mentors, beginning with my parents, paved the way for their children to become bigger than de facto slavery, Jim Crow, and racism—even when there seemed to be no way out.

I imagined that as the racist gang beat my father's adolescent back until he was unconscious, everything turned black. At that moment, he must have determined it was better to die right than to live wrong. For the sake of doing what he thought was right, he endangered his own family's holdings and their lives in order to warn other blacks of the racist threats to take their farms and cattle. In spite of that, he survived and thrived! How many future generations were helped by the deeds of one man?

I discovered my father married his first wife, Fannie Pollard, on February 18, 1899. Census records showed that he and his new wife lived in Daphne, Alabama, and that he worked for the railroad company for fifty cents a day. He could heave a crosstie onto his shoulder, carry it to the rails, drive the spikes home, and lead other men to do the same. That combination of strength and leadership quickly earned him a promotion to foreman. From that day, he received and earned a dollar a day for such backbreaking labor.

Could such information affect the reshaping of Tuskegee?

After he saved enough money, my father bought his first forty acres of land in Loxley, Alabama. Eventually, he quit the railroad to focus on his farm and turpentine business. One of his coworkers was dumbfounded by the decision he made to quit such a good job.

"Mr. Jenkins, why you give up this job? It's a dollar a day!"

"If I'm worth that much to *them*, I'm worth a lot more to *me*," he answered.

Starting with the money he earned from that first forty acres, my father began his career as a plantation owner and entrepreneur. He worked hard and acquired more land, adding to those forty acres in Loxley bit by bit. Soon, he was raising hogs and cattle and growing sweet potatoes, white potatoes, corn, sugarcane, and soybeans. He built a distillation plant and converted raw rosin harvested from pine trees into turpentine and other commercial products.

He built a pulpwood operation, selling wood for conversion to paper. He developed a syrup processing operation to convert sugarcane into table syrup. He constructed a private electrical system with generators and twenty large batteries to provide electricity for his general store, home, and many other needs.

On March 7, 1919, my father's wife of twenty years died, leaving him a widower with no children at the age of forty-five. He met my mother, a devoted teacher named Amelia Taylor, in nearby Daphne, Alabama. I don't know how they met, only that they were both active members of the community. My father was one of the founders and deacons of Mt. Aide Baptist Church in Loxley, and it was only a matter of time before he and my mother crossed paths and got married.

My mother always reminded her children that my father stood out among other men whenever he went into town. His clothes were always cleaned and pressed, and his manner was confident. He was respectful and tipped his hat. He made a good name for himself, and others spoke well of him.

People spoke well of my mother too. She was twenty years younger than my father, but she was mature, bright, diligent, and honest.

Amelia Taylor Jenkins

My parents shared the same dreams. All my older sisters and brothers said they saw the future as a vast, modern farm, a cradle of innovation and good values with which to nurture and inspire their ten children. My three sisters and six brothers and I were recipients of their dreams.

"You must have high standards in life," my mother often said. "Whatever you do, be the best you can be."

I've carried those words with me my entire life because the family farm embodied those values even before I was born. And when I came along, everywhere I looked, I saw ingenuity and the reflection of a job well done. The fences stood tall, and not one single creosote post was out of place. The fields were tilled, and no equipment was broken or left in disarray.

The processing plants buzzed with such efficiency that other farmers in the area brought their sugarcane to us for processing. We had a gas station outside our general store and an in-store smokehouse for our meats.

By focusing on finding a need and filling it—with good, honest service—the Jenkins' family became one of the most influential farmers in the region. Farmers came from near and far to observe our practices and apply them on their farms, and we were happy to share the knowledge. Farmers with higher than expected crop yields would often contract with us to complete their harvests. These interactions taught me that sharing knowledge and providing community service were good strategies for business.

My parents laid down great management and business ethics for their children to follow. They taught us how important their employees were to the family enterprise. They employed all races, even former inmates, and German prisoners of World War II who were housed in a military compound near our farm. My parents made sure the workers all had decent lodging and built a housing development called Jenkins Quarters. They rented thirty homes for fair prices to trusted employees.

HARD WORK, MODERN METHODS MAKE JENKINS FARM SUCCESS

THE FORMULA for the success of the Jenkins family is a simple one. It consists of long hours of hard work plus the employment of the latest proved scientific methods of farming. During planting and harvesting seasons, the brothers sometimes work all night, using the headlights of their farm machinery for illumination. Their usual working day during the busy season is 18 hours. Even in slack seasons they put in nine hours a day.

The formula has paid off with such a tremendous success that most of the whites in the area are amazed. Some of them refuse to believe that the modern, well-kept farm really belongs to Negroes.

Once a white man stopped at the small store operated by the Jenkinses and asked Mrs. Amelia Jenkins where "the lady of the house" was.

"I'm the lady of the house," she told him.

"Maybe your name is Jenkins," he said, "but you are not the one I want to see."

"There's another one over at the big house," she told him—referring to her 7-room home where her daughter-in-law, Helen Jenkins, was then staying.

The white man headed for the big house and Mrs. Jenkins went to the telephone to tell Helen to answer the door and say that she was Mrs. Jenkins. Helen did as she was told and the flabbergasted white man exclaimed, "You are Mrs. Jenkins!"

"Yes," Helen said sweetly. "Of course if you want the other one, she's at the store. There are only two."

Another white man stopped by and asked Hilliard where he could find Mr. Jenkins.

"That's me," Hilliard told him.

"Now listen here, boy," the white man said, "I know you're kidding me. Let me see the man who owns the house."

Jenkins got so angry that he ordered the man off the farm—and he went.

White residents in Baldwin County, aware of the tremendous influence which the Jenkins have with Negroes, frequently ask them to help put over important campaigns. This year, when the county held an all-out blood drive, Mrs. Jenkins was delegated to publicize it among Negroes. She did, on the condition that Negroes would not be segregated at the Red Cross station. They were not. Remarked one white Alabaman: "Everybody here knows there's no difference between white and colored blood. But it takes people like the Jenkinses to make us really aware of it."

Pleasant-faced Mrs. Amelia Jenkins has appearance that belies her age (59) and years of back-breaking toil which led to success.

Welding broken tool, Shelley Jenkins wears helmet to protect face from sparks. Family cuts cost of machinery upkeep by doing most of own repair work right on farm.

Boss of hired hands is personable manager Samuel Jenkins. A war veteran, he studied scientific farming, sometimes supervises 100 employees.

I learned from my parents' model of doing business—treat others the way you want to be treated. Though my parents didn't discriminate, they were not naïve. They realized that fair practices would not entirely stop hate and discrimination. Yet they refused to hate or discriminate themselves, even when they had good reason.

As an example, they rented land thick with pine trees in several locations beyond Loxley for their turpentine business. At one site, racist whites set fires to the trees. My parents decided retaliation would be a waste of energy and hired white people from the surrounding areas to share the work.

"They did the chipping, and we did the dipping," my brother Samuel always said.

The fires ceased. My parents turned a bad situation into something good. By their example, they taught us to be fearless in our interactions with others, black or white.

One night, a group of white men came knocking on the front door. Being no fool, my father kept the doors locked.

"Who is it?" he asked.

"The bread man's truck is bogged down in the creek up the road. We need you and your mule team to pull him out," one of the men said.

My father huddled with my mother, and they agreed that whatever the men needed could wait until daylight. They figured the men were Ku Klux Klan.

"I'll help you at first light," my father answered.

"Throw on something and get out here," the voice demanded.

Like most black farmers, my father slept with a loaded double-barrel shotgun above his bed. He turned off the lights, walked into the bedroom to get his gun, and stepped out onto the porch. As soon as he fired the first blast into the air, the men scrambled off his property.

There was no need to fire the second barrel.

Whenever my older sisters and brothers recalled my father's courage that night, I felt strong and fearless. I grew up on those stories long before I was old enough to understand their deep implications back in the '60s. As a grown man, those memories brought the understanding of how Tuskegee deserved my sacrifice to help pull them through a rough time in a new century. I had learned long ago how to deal with difficulty: head on.

In 1944, after my brother Samuel returned from World War II, a local farmer who did business with us told him that he had been a Ku Klux Klan member. He confessed that he had attended a meeting on the night Klansmen plotted to sabotage the Jenkins' farm or kill my dad. That man gave the Klansmen a warning: "If you set foot on the Jenkins' farm, you gonna go home with fewer men than you started with."

I always remembered that story when I came face to face with danger. "Never start a fight, but you have my permission to finish it."

I also remember the story about the generosity my father showed his family. Around 1930, he was finally able to return to Mississippi and bring his sister Charity to Baldwin County, along with her family: Maggie, Ella, and James. It must have been fulfilling for him to return to Mississippi as a prosperous businessman, where he had faced almost certain death. He also brought other relatives from one of the most racist areas of Mississippi to Baldwin County. It wasn't perfect, but it was without question a better place for them to live.

He built a home for his sister's family near ours, and my cousin James and I worked together milking cows at five o'clock every morning from the age of five. We adopted him as our brother.

I still talk to James every now and then. He always says he wouldn't be the man he is today if it hadn't been for my mother. He was spoiled and unruly when he came to live with us, but my mother quickly brought him into line. As a teacher, she was pretty good at keeping tykes and teens in order. James became a great team player after learning my mother's favorite phrase: "No slacking."

To gather and sustain a great harvest requires daily diligence. There's no relaxing on a farm, only action and reaction. You plant, tend the soil, harvest, and cycle crops from one season to the next. The Jenkins' children, blood relations, adopted children, and others in the community all learned how hard work produced plentiful harvests and connected us with the soil.

> *The soil is the connector of lives, the source and destination of all.*

—Wendell Barry

CHAPTER 4

The Game Plan

By 1935, my parents had considerable debt. They had accepted the responsibility of working the farm, feeding, clothing, and educating their children, and then tragedy struck. My father died of a heart attack.

His untimely death left my mother with nine children and a tenth on the way—my youngest sister, Johnetta. Ten thousand dollars in debt, ten children to feed, and the most recent acquisition of seven hundred acres of undeveloped land loomed over her head.

Growing up with that story, I learned that success seldom comes easy. Most often, it takes strife to become tough enough to stand under the pressure. During our strife, my mother gave her children the greatest gift. She showed us how to persevere in the face of great adversity. She put us all to work.

In a time when few women were educated, my mother had studied science at the Tuskegee Institute under the famous botanist and inventor Dr. George Washington Carver. Just as my father had refused to wilt during his darkest hours, she did the same. She called all her children inside and gathered us around her in the high-backed rocking chair.

"Listen, you all, we're going to stick together. We're going to work hard and grow this farm." She paused and looked at each of us.

"Your daddy and I had big plans. We're going to carry them out. We're going to make something of ourselves."

She stood up. "Now let's put our shoulders to the wheel and push together."

What those words meant was that I had to get up at five o'clock in the morning at age five. Those words touched our entire family for a lifetime.

As time passed, she did whatever it took to implement the tasks assigned to us. She turned our struggle into a character-building experience and instilled deep values of setting goals and figuring out a game plan to reach them. Day in and day out, she taught us that a goal is a useless dream until you have a game plan to make it a reality. She taught us to "plan your work and work your plan."

When I was three, my mother assigned me to pick up pecans that fell from the trees. At four, I lugged water to the animals, and at five, I milked the cows every morning at five o'clock. By seven, I was driving a field truck. I would carefully inch the truck forward while the field hands loaded sacks of sweet potatoes and corn into the truck beds.

When I turned eight, I drove tractors. I set the plows and tilled the soil. I carried my lunch to the field and took one fifteen-minute break to eat. I'd drive that tractor all day, and by seven or eight at night, when I finally shut it down, the engine looked as red as fire.

All my mother's children rose every morning between 4:00 and 5:00 a.m. I get up around that time to this very day. We all knew what our duties were and we did them without fuss or fail. There was no compromise or arguing about it. We knew the cost of getting up late and having another family member wake us up. That strong work ethic was the foundation of our character.

Once, I overheard a neighbor telling my mother she was going to work her kids to death.

She just laughed. "It's good for them," she said.

Our mother entrusted us with responsibilities that were vital to our family's survival and instrumental to our success. We had pigs, cows, horses, and chickens to feed. The troughs had to be filled on schedule. If we needed chickens to eat for dinner, we'd grab a couple from the coop.

With $40,000 worth of farm machinery, Mrs. Amelia Jenkins and her family own one of the richest farms in Alabama. Working the 1,052-acre family farm for Mrs. Jenkins, four of her sons use every modern device to make the land among the most productive in the state. The sons are (left to right) Samuel, John, Hilliard and Shelley.

ALABAMA'S RICHEST FARM FAMILY

Amelia Jenkins and sons gross more than $130,000 yearly on huge 1,052-acre property

IN LOXLEY, ALABAMA, 27 years ago, Mrs. Amelia Jenkins, a sturdily-built dark-skinned woman with powerful hands and a husky voice, scooped up a fistful of loose brown topsoil near the family's debt-ridden turpentine farm in Baldwin County. Looking at yellowish earth beneath it, she thoughtfully told her husband, "It's good potato land, John, and it could make us wealthy."

While John Jenkins Sr., never lived to see the dream materialize, his wife did. Today, she and their 10 children are the owners of 1,052 acres of some of the South's best timber and farm land. Quiet, proud, hard-working people with solemn faces, the Jenkinses own perhaps the richest Negro farm in the state,

and are ranked among its biggest agriculturists, "white or colored," as Southerners say. During 1952, one of their bumper years, they grossed over $130,000 from the sale of vegetables, cotton, hogs and cattle. Biggest single crop was Irish potatoes, which alone brought them over $95,000. By marketing 106 head of fine Aberdeen Angus and Hereford feeder steers, they earned over $22,000. Cotton was one of their smaller crops. With only 40 acres of it, they made $6,668.

This year, having increased the cultivated land from 507 to 960 acres, and having added yet another major crop—soy beans—the Jenkins clan expects an even greater income.

Their land stretches as far as the eye can

see, but the Jenkinses still plan to buy more. Mrs. Amelia Jenkins says it was her dream to see her children become secure and self-sufficient, and this is the culmination of her plans. Her son, Hilliard, is even more ambitious. Each year, he says, he will buy more land for cultivation. When he has 2,000, maybe 3,000 acres, then and only then, he says, will he be satisfied. "When a man has soil, he has a future," Hilliard says.

"There is no excuse for Negroes here not having anything," says Hilliard Jenkins, "because the land is good and will respond to the hands of men who are not afraid to work. And one thing which nobody will ever accuse us of is being lazy."

There's no room for slackers on a farm. My mother's children learned that laziness at any stage in the growing season could ruin an entire crop, which explains why so many kids with farming backgrounds thrive as adults and as professionals.

Every day, we saw my mother lead by example, with both hired workers and her own children. She helped cut down trees and snake logs out of the woods with mule teams. She chopped cotton, managed the store and the house, and raised ten kids. There wasn't an ounce of slack in my mother, and she didn't tolerate it in her children.

I walked three miles to and from elementary school every day. In high school, I alternated school days to work on the farm—two days one week and three days the next. But despite my absences, I was always an honor student. By today's child labor laws, my mother would have been fined or worse. And while I strongly support child labor laws, I view my own childhood experience as a gift.

Positive associations with hard work and pride in a job well done are among the greatest gifts my mother gave us. I took seriously the early experience of clearing trees, turning the soil, planting seeds, and seeing things grow as a result of my diligence, hard work, and perseverance.

The ultimate harvest was character.

"You all stay close together, you hear?" my mother would tell us.

And we did. The Jenkins' kids stayed close. I did everything with my brothers and sisters. We worked and studied together. We went to church and double-dated. And we were always there for each other. I cannot stress how important unconditional love was during my childhood.

It's a tough thing for children to lose a parent at any age, but because of my mother's guidance and the close bond our family developed, we built a foundation of love and support.

In my younger years, the thought of such love would bring tears of joy to my eyes.

CHAPTER 5

❖❖❖

My Mother, Plantation Boss

Like the rich soil on our farm, my upbringing was rooted in rich and edifying values, which were reflected on the farm and in our home. My mother worked both our minds and our bodies. She taught us to grow gardens during the day and assigned book reports at night, which we gave at the dinner table for the family. She taught us the morality of achievement by hard work.

I can still hear her voice: "There's no right way to do wrong!"

My oldest brother, John Wesley Jenkins Jr., is a perfect example of my mother's belief in doing the best you can with what you have. He was born so small he fit in an oatmeal box. He suffered from rickets throughout his childhood and had to wear cumbersome metal braces. He was also a juvenile diabetic.

Those ailments hindered his physical development and made it difficult for him to work the land, but it didn't stop him from contributing to the family business. He didn't have brawn, so he cultivated his brain. He earned his BS and MS from Tennessee State University and tended to all the bookkeeping and accounting for the business.

At the age of forty, he died in a car crash, but I will remember him always for making the most with what he had.

Every Sunday morning, my mother would gather us around the breakfast table and talk about life. She spoke of integrity, values, setting goals, success, honesty, discipline, hard work, getting along with people, and finding a lifetime mate. She'd always include a thoughtful prayer that expressed thanks and hope for the future.

"If you want to be successful, your word is your bond. If you tell a person that you are going to do something, do it. Take pride in everything you do. If the job must be done, do it well. Be careful about the friends you choose. Make sure their values are consistent with yours."

Though I never knew my father personally, my mother and siblings kept his values and memory alive. I saw the legacy of his innovative spirit and his refusal to see limits. Before the Rural Electrification Act, my father wired our farm with electricity. He didn't live to see its benefits, but all the neighbors were able to come around to hear Joe Louis fights on our radio. His innovation taught me to never put limits on what I could do. Although blacks comprised only ten percent of Baldwin County, our family was one of the five most influential families in the county.

By the early 1950s, we'd wiped our debt off the bank ledgers, and the farm was booming. We now had about one thousand acres. The hard work was paying off. More than solvent, we were profitable, and that success did not go unnoticed.

In 1952, our farm won the Tuskegee Institute's annual National Family Farm Award. *Ebony* magazine wrote that we were "Alabama's most successful black farm family."

Allen Rankin wrote in the Alabama journal how the Jenkins brothers looked like a "commando attack," the objective being to take a potato field instead of a beachhead. "Up at four every morning, the Jenkins' sons are often still working in the fields long after nightfall."

Rankin added that he had not seen such organized hustle and bustle since the building of the B-29 airstrips in the Pacific.

Rankin's article stressed how people in Baldwin County trusted and respected the Jenkins' name. Everybody knew the word of a Jenkins was solid as oak. One day when I was a child, I was riding with my mother who was driving at what seemed like ninety miles an hour.

We heard a siren behind us. My mother pulled over and a rock flew up and hit the white policeman's car.

My mother stuck her head out of the window. "Why did you stop me?"

I heard the policeman say, "I'm sorry, Mrs. Jenkins. I didn't know that was you. Go ahead on."

That's when I realized how much the Jenkins' family reputation was respected.

Beyond the prestige of our farm and the many successes my siblings and I achieved, one of my fondest memories of life on the farm was Jubilee in the summer when the sun glistened on the sand and the wind blew a warm breeze from the gulf to the bay. We'd pull a bounty of seafood out of the gulf and have huge cookouts. I remember green and gold crops at harvest time and how my mom and sisters would load up the truck with food and roll our general store into the field during lunchtime.

Sundays were always great days for our family. We'd rise early and get dressed in our church clothes. Our trucks were equipped with ladders and benches so people without transportation could climb in and ride with us to church. Folks would walk miles to our store to catch a ride. We became known for kindness at that gathering place. My mother would give out produce to the community.

Every year, white tramps with little more than the clothes on their backs would stop on their way to Florida for the winter. My mother would give them food. At other times, gypsy women would come around, and she'd feed them too. She'd often tell me to take a bag of food to someone nearby or send my brothers and me to pull someone out of a ditch.

As a kid, I wondered why my mother would give away so much—why she had us to do for others without getting anything in return.

Whenever I asked her, she'd only say, "One day, you'll understand."

Today, I understand.

Giving is where the joy comes from. If you can give and by giving make another person's life a little easier, you're making the world a better place. People who hoard things they could share never seem to know real joy or true success.

Years ago, a writer wanted to publish a national story on my family to explore why all the children were successful. Although we declined requests for interviews, we learned about another prolific Jenkins' family line that still existed in Shuqualak, Mississippi. After many years, we reconnected with Dr. Velma Hill Jenkins, a member of the extended Jenkins' family. She was serving as the mayor of Shuqualak, Mississippi. Such were my father's roots.

On July 7 and 8, 1989, the Jenkins gathered in Shuqualak for a family reunion.

What a pleasure it was to find that large, wonderful extended family of ours, who I now consider the "Lost Tribe."

Though my dad was dealt the horrible fate of nearly being killed by the KKK, he never forgot his values or his resolve to live as a proud, free American.

Together, my parents passed those elements into the hearts and minds of my siblings and me like unbending steel rods. My father's family in Mississippi had given him solid values, and he shared them with all his children, and through them, his children's children and beyond. Though he found himself alone in Alabama without a cent to his name, his parents had given him the wisdom to survive and succeed.

I have observed again and again that the difference between families that succeed versus those that struggle is largely determined by inherited legacies. By this, I mean how parents and grandparents instill values, wisdom, and the power of planning and pursuing ethical goals.

This legacy of inherited values, planning, and goals made all the difference for me. Those values are in my DNA.

My brother Levaughn says the only thing our mother didn't teach us was how to fail, and he was right. Our parents gave us an inherited vision of the United States where we could succeed in the face of enormous challenges if we kept our minds clear of immoral thoughts and pursued ethical goals.

Positive possibilities always lay just ahead. When Levaughn was passed over for promotion nine times, he only worked harder, and eventually, he was promoted to colonel in the US Air Force.

He admits that were it not for his positive childhood training that kept him from giving in to hate and anger, he might not have persevered amid the military's institutional racism that had for so long denied him the rank he deserved.

My older sister Connie Jenkins-Harper founded an award-winning organization, the Central Alabama Opportunities Industrialization Center, Inc. (OIC), in Montgomery, Alabama. Were it not for her grit, determination, and persistence in dealing with Alabama governor George Wallace, Connie's OIC would not exist today, still providing benefits to that community. Had Connie given up on herself, her vision, and on Wallace, many homes and shopping centers would never have been built in Montgomery. For that feat, a school was named after her, training welfare recipients to work and obtain high-paying jobs in the private sector.

Jimmy Faulkner, state senator and one of Alabama's powerful political brokers said, "Practically everybody in central Alabama knows Connie Jenkins-Harper and calls her by her first name."

Just one generation removed from the shackles of slavery, my parents led our family from a penniless existence to a thriving family farm enterprise in a supportive community. Their accomplishment still amazes me.

Equally astounding is that the ten children of John Wesley and Amelia Jenkins have enlarged their parents' vision and instilled their values, wisdom, and work ethic into future generations.

◄◄►►

John Wesley Jenkins's father, Hilliard Jenkins, was born into slavery. John Wesley would name his second son Hilliard, after his father, and rather than work on a plantation, his son would run one. Along with my mother, Hilliard managed the entire Jenkins Farm Enterprise and would go on to have a street and a college scholarship named after him. My brother Samuel served as head of the Longshoreman's Union and was the first black county commissioner in Baldwin County, Alabama. He was probably the most influential elected official in the county.

In July 2012, county officials honored Samuel for his service by naming a stretch of US Highway 90 after him. The section of I-90 from Baldwin County 13 to Alabama 181 is now the Samuel Jenkins Sr. Highway.

A common thread runs through the lives of every member of my family—a devotion to service and humanitarianism. We make a practice of helping those less fortunate.

My sisters Azalee and Johnetta were both nurses. My brother Shelly had a distinguished career as an electrician and longshoreman in Mobile, Alabama. My brother Joyful, like Levaughn, was a Tuskegee Airman. Joyful was killed in Thailand during the Vietnam War while flying tankers to refuel air force bombers.

Matthew Jenkins continues family's legacy of greatness

There is nothing more interesting than people.

And Baldwin is fortunate to have a great supply of fine people whose successes deserve to be recorded .... particularly some excellent families.

And I enjoy knowing and writing about some of these. Here goes for a highly successful and civic minded family.

In fact, I would have to say that this family is one of the top families in Baldwin County.

I am talking about the Jenkins family of Belforest and Daphne, the children of the late Amelia T. Jenkins, who came here many years ago with her husband from Mississippi.

The children totaled 10, of which four boys and three girls are still living.

Space does not permit mentioning all of them, but many people in the county already know Samuel Jenkins, who is one of the fine members of our good County Commission. There is not a more dedicated, hard-working public official to be found.

In times past, I have written about Connie Jenkins Harper, who has made a great name for herself and is executive director of Central Alabama Opportunities Industrialization Center Inc., of Montgomery. Practically everyone in central Alabama knows Connie and calls her by name.

One of her closest friends and admirers was the late Gov. George C. Wallace. She returned the affections because George had helped in some of her many projects that she has continually been successful in to serve poor and underprivileged people. She has gotten hundreds of jobs for people in her area and continues to be successful in her endeavors, even though her health is not as good as it once was.

She has been the recipient of many honors, newspapers and magazine articles.

Today, I want to talk to you about the youngest member of the family, Dr. Matthew Jenkins, who is a successful veterinarian-turned real estate magnate and who has given millions to higher education.

He was the subject of a main article, with his picture on the front cover of *Pulse* magazine, a

Jimmy Faulkner
Mumblings

nationally distributed periodical.

Dr. Jenkins has sought and achieved great accomplishments.

The magazine states, "Dr. Matthew Jenkins parlayed an old-fashioned Alabama upbringing and education into a successful California veterinary medical practice — a practice which he sold in 1979, but which is still paying dividends 20 years later through the efforts of his successors.

"For some, that might have been a career itself — a lifetime accomplishment of full-filling a dream, but for Dr. Jenkins, who was 45 when he sold the business, he was just getting started.

"He went on to create an unusually successful real estate investment and property management enterprise and then carried on in his family tradition of 'paying back' to the community, generally by funding educational projects, programs, scholarships, organizations, institutions and individuals."

When graduating from high school, his mother encouraged him to go to Tuskeegee and he asked a brother, already in classes there, what was "the hardest stuff they got." His brother told him "a lot of guys flunk out of veterinary medicine" ... he decided that was the course he wanted.

As a member of the U.S. Air Force, he was promoted to captain and sent to Greenland. While there, he discovered a rabies problem in 1958 and became the first person to establish a disease eradication program against rabies in that country and received much recognition for it, including an article published in 1961 in the *Journal of the American*

Veterinary Medical Association.

According to the article, he has given millions of dollars to higher education and hundreds of scholarships to deserving students. He has also served on the board of several universities.

He established a real estate company, S.D.D. Enterprises, Inc., which now owns 11 mobile home parks in six states, with more than 3,500 units and has paid his investors some $16 million to date.

He said, "I am a believer in education. You can expose a person to education, give a person some bait and a fishing pole and let him go catch his own fish."

Dr. Jenkins and his wife, Roberta, make their home in Long Beach, Calif., and he has given deep consideration to turning some of his real estate investment knowledge to his home county of Baldwin.

"We've got one property that looks like a city, with a shopping center, swimming pool, fishing lake, and we are going to build a retirement village in Alabama," he said. He added, "the project will include 1,200 units with 3,500 people living here."

He stated, "my dad was born in Mississippi and died when I was 2 years old in 1935." But he further states he left his family a legacy, not only in the 300-acre plantation he bought in the Belforest community, but in family values that have remained with all brothers and sisters. He states, "we all learned to work hard. We discussed values and discipline around the family table."

Dr. Jenkins has also been active in politics and was a personal friend and major fund raiser for former Los Angeles Mayor Tom Bradley, who died last month.

When asked what message he had to give students he said, "they can go as far in life as they envision that they can, with the only impediment being their own lack of vision."

Amelia Jenkins raised quite a family. A book should be written about it.

See you again soon, I hope.

Jimmy Faulkner of Bay Minette is a former newspaper publisher, state senator, and gubernatorial candidate.

Each of us, my wife, my siblings, and myself, in our own way, have always lived a life of service. When you give to others, you share a part of your soul. The signs, plaques, and awards my family has received are only symbols of that which we leave for others.

A road that ran along our family farm in Loxley was renamed Jenkins Farm Road, affirming the success of my family's farm. It is a tribute to the dream my mother and father planned and actualized.

The section of US 90 named for Samuel connects with Jenkins Farm Road, which connects to Hilliard Jenkins Road, which connects to the I-10. In Mobile, the I-10 traveling west to California connects with I-65, which leads to Montgomery, Alabama, where the school named for Connie is located. Interstate 65 connects to I-10 and passes the Matthew and Roberta Jenkins Courtyard at the Drucker School of Business at Claremont Graduate University in Claremont, California, then proceeds west where my home overlooks the Pacific Ocean.

I live far away from Baldwin County today, but I visit often and still know the roads like the back of my hand, all which lead back to the rich soil and culturally wealthy people who gave me my start.

CHAPTER 6

Lessons from Unwanted Bulls and Unwanted Crops

Tuskegee had played a significant role in my journey from Alabama to California, so naturally, I paused to consider how I could give back to an institution where I found such support and trust.

Over the years, my family kept a good relationship with the Malbis Greek Colony. The Malbis' family restaurant would give us their food scraps to feed our hogs, and we in turn helped other farmers harvest their crops. We all shared expertise, traded goods, and found ourselves thriving more as a community than a bunch of insular individuals. One farmer's refuse was another farmer's resource.

A great example of fruitful exchange was the baby bulls we raised. We lived near the Thomas Dairy farm, which didn't want most of its male calves. Dairy farmers only needed one bull for every forty or fifty cows. So we purchased the male calves from Thomas Dairy for one dollar each. That meant we had fifteen to twenty baby bulls at any given time, and I was in charge of bottle-feeding them until they were big enough to eat solid food.

We dewormed the bulls and castrated them, and when they were old enough, we took them to market and made a nice profit. It turned into a great little side business—a profit center of its own. From that early experience, I learned there were lots of things that others might not need or want that could nonetheless be turned into something of value.

We applied that principle to everything we did, from saving and earning to undervalued crops.

During harvest season, we took the best ears of corn and shipped them to New York and Chicago for a good price but were always left with a number of smaller ears that were not saleable. So we hauled silage machines out to the cornfields and ground up all those little ears and their stalks. The machines blew the chopped corn bits into our truck beds, and we dumped it all in our silos, along with other undervalued crops we hauled in from our fields and surrounding farms. In time, that mixture would ferment into meal that we mixed with cottonseed and mineral supplements to feed our cattle. We didn't waste anything.

I learned that you can take throwaway animals and crops and put them together to turn a handsome profit. What I'm getting at is how to spot creative possibilities—finding resources that other people might not see or consider. Business people are always talking about finding a niche. I turned those one-dollar bulls into more stock, and the undervalued crops were used to fatten them up.

Too often, people look for big and grandiose business opportunities, but good niche opportunities are often humbler as well as more practical. The opportunities are usually right in front of you. Most niche business ideas are small, focused, and accommodate the marketplace.

I loved growing up on the farm and wouldn't trade the experience for anything. You start with nothing but a dirt field, and you work the earth. You till the soil, plant the seeds, and nurse them along. You run a tractor and a cultivator along the various rows, and when harvest comes, that field looks like a beautiful painting. It makes you feel good inside. It's pure pride to turn dirt into something that magnificent.

And the next season, you do it all again.

Many people have said to me, "Man, I wouldn't want to work on a farm like that."

But I loved it. There's nothing like working the land that connects you to this earth.

That's the reason I didn't want to go to college. I loved life on the farm. I never looked at it as work. I was just having fun. I loved going out and checking on the crops, tending to the animals, and running the machines.

Maybe if I had come from some rundown little farm, I would have felt a different way. But we had one of the best farms in the county. We had a white picket fence that we regularly touched up with fresh paint. We lived right off US Highway 90, a route heading to Florida.

We posted a tall sign: "Jenkins Farm."

People driving along the highway would often stop to take pictures of it.

Back when I was about fourteen years old, my brothers, Shelly and Hilliard, and I were clearing new ground, which meant we were chopping down trees and digging up the roots so we had more land for crops. We didn't have skip loaders back then, so this was hard work.

I'll never forget one day when I was as sick as a farm dog. Being part of a culture of hard work, we were expected to press on no matter what, that's what I usually did. But on that day, I was just too sick to keep working. My brothers thought I was slacking off and they laid a fierce whipping on me.

I was hurt, sick, and angry, and I stormed back to the house and grabbed the double-barreled shotgun, replacing the #8 shells we used to kill birds and replaced them with double ought, powerful enough to blow a hole in a man's chest the size of his fist.

I didn't hesitate. I walked straight for the cornfield where I knew my brothers could not see me. I cocked the gun just as I reached the cornfield, about to disappear from sight.

It was at that moment I heard the voice of my mother. I didn't know where she came from so suddenly, but that's something a mother does well. She shows up where she's needed.

"Where you going with that gun, Matthew?"

I turned to face the woman who gave birth to me. "I'm going to kill Shelly and Hilliard," I answered. And I was too.

She looked calm, but I can only imagine what she was thinking.

"Give me that gun," she said calmly.

I didn't argue.

I held out the gun, and she took it from me with a firm hand. "Go on in the house now," she said.

In the following days, I'm sure she spoke to Shelley and Hilliard about the incident, but neither brother nor my mom ever mentioned it to me. They never tried to beat me again either.

Reflecting on that moment now gives me a chill. Had my mother not stopped me, I'm certain I would have killed my brothers because I was about as mad as I've ever been. A tragedy like that could have killed all the family's dreams and plagued us with a terrible incident of blood and violence. Thinking about that in light of today's rampant gun violence spotlights three realities:

One—had my mother not caught me with that gun, the trajectory of my life and my family's lives would have been markedly different.

Two—my mother's steady and involved parenting gave all my brothers and sisters a strong moral grounding, but it was entirely possible that my mother could have been busy with a customer when I stalked into the cornfield, gun cocked and ready. I realize how lucky I was that my mother saw me that day. She gave me life, and she saved my life.

That said, I realize no parent is perfect, and each generation should refine its own parenting skills. I think my mother probably should have gathered the three of us together to talk things over.

Violence is too often a reality in the lives of our children, so it's incumbent upon us as parents to discuss alternatives to violence.

Three—my shotgun incident highlights that my close call with a gun was not so different from most gun-related tragedies. I was an angry young man with easy access to a gun. Easy access to guns promotes gun violence.

I reject the National Rifle Association's slogan that "Guns don't kill people, people kill people." Sure, it takes a human being to pull the trigger, but that ignores the reality that people in a state of passion are only thinking about the moment—consequences are the furthest thing from their minds. That's why anger and access to guns are a deadly combination for human life.

TIME magazine recently published a feature article entitled "How the Gun Won."

The article outlines how gun laws have lapsed over the last two decades. Shortly before the time of this writing, James Holmes went on a notorious murder spree in Aurora, Colorado, killing twelve people in a movie theater and wounding many others. I understand that it is impossible to stop every madman from taking violent actions. But I don't think buying semiautomatic rifles, shotguns, handguns, and six thousand rounds of ammunition should have been as easy for Holmes as ordering a book online.

Then like salt in a painful wound, twenty-year-old Adam Lanza murdered twenty beautiful children and six adults at Sandy Hook Elementary School in Newtown, Connecticut—twenty first-graders.

The nation was overwhelmed with grief, but in response to that tragedy, NRA executive vice president Wayne LaPierre called for armed guards to be stationed in every school in the country. LaPierre said, "The only thing that stops a bad guy with a gun is a good guy with a gun."

Rather than take any responsibility for the loosest gun laws in years—laws that allow mentally unstable people to purchase high-powered rifles, hundred-round magazines, and thousands of rounds of ammunition—the NRA chose to distort the issue. An important and complex social issue was reduced to a cartoonish zero-sum game. Children had been murdered, and all the NRA could think about was finding new ways to sell guns.

I am chastened to look back on how vulnerable I was in that moment of fourteen-year-old rage. And I know that adolescence and early adulthood have grown far more confusing for today's youth than it was for me. I never thought I'd see the day when young people and grown men are constantly engaged with video games that simulate bloody killings and murderous rampages.

Yet impressionable young people spend hours upon hours playing bloody murder games, and that troubles me greatly. There are video games that simulate crimes and sexual violence against women. How can such video games be used to teach positive things, rather than murder, rape, and crime simulators?

I am a fierce defender of freedom of speech, and I understand that upholding liberty requires tolerance for the expression of others with whom I disagree, however repugnant I find their views. I do not agree with video games and other media that encourage cruelty, brutality, and violence, but I can't stop others from making and selling them.

I can, however, urge my family members and other parents to be vigilant about what's occupying the minds of their children.

Children are a precious resource, and we need to nurture them with as much care and diligence as a farmer nursing his crops from the soil.

People who reinforce their minds with wholesome and pro-social thoughts will ultimately act in a positive manner. And the inverse is true, as well: people who reinforce their minds with violent and antisocial thoughts are more likely to become a negative force in society. Awareness of this is particularly important in the twenty-first century when the average person spends hours each day staring into their phones, computers, and televisions. What you see is what you get.

To bring it full circle, I believe parents need to make sure they never turn away from the viewing habits of their children or themselves. They need to talk to their kids about violence and be constantly mindful of the digital media that young, impressionable minds consume.

I also believe elected officials need to stop goldbricking on guns. Having the right to bear arms should not mean easy access to dangerous weapons. I say this as someone who once held such a weapon and nearly made the worst mistake of my life.

I learned that day that I should always think things through, no matter what pressure or distractions come my way.

CHAPTER 7

◦⟨⟨⟨❈⟩⟩⟩◦

The Tuskegee Circle: From Loxley Elementary to Tuskegee University

As a young boy, I learned and accepted that, as a minority in the United States, I would have to work harder than a white person to succeed. From experiencing those teachings, I was able to make peace with the inequity. My parents taught me to resist anger and bitterness that usually came along with unjust acts, because to embrace them would make matters worse.

As a result, I decided to work twice as hard as the average person to reach my goals. Working from dawn till dusk on the farm conditioned me to achieve my purpose in almost any circumstance. Challenges always showed up and always will, but they taught me to look and work toward the future I desired and not react to how I felt about them in the moment.

Back in 1901, state lawmakers altered the Alabama constitution with new laws that mandated segregation of public schools. The one-drop rule was instituted—meaning students with any fraction of African American blood would be labeled "colored." Colored people were required to enroll in segregated schools. Those segregated schools were underfunded and typically housed in substandard facilities. That was the character of the Deep South.

Fortunately, in the face of this rampant inequality, education visionaries and philanthropists extended a vital learning lifeline to me, my siblings, and my fellow students in Baldwin County and throughout the south. I was provided a nurturing environment to get a better education than most of the surrounding southern communities. I credit our rich culture of learning to what I consider "The Tuskegee Circle."

The Tuskegee Circle started at Loxley Colored School, where I attended first through sixth grades. The construction of that elementary school was financed by the Rosenwald Fund, which was established by Julius Rosenwald, one of the founders of Sears, Roebuck and Company and who was one of the wealthiest Americans during my youth.

In May 1911, Rosenwald met with Booker T. Washington, founder of the Tuskegee Institute, to discuss ways to "promote the well-being of colored people in America."

Years ahead of other white liberals, Rosenwald joined the Tuskegee Board of Directors and, working with Booker T. Washington, launched a rural school-building initiative that would serve the educational needs of "663,615 students in 883 counties of fifteen states," according to the National Trust for Historic Preservation, which gave the Rosenwald Schools a national treasure designation in 2011, one hundred years later.

Washington and Rosenwald understood that schools were vehicles for the goals of American democracy. Schools don't guarantee success, but social and financial stability accompanied by good schools and educational opportunities offer the best chance for developing productive people.

Because of school segregation, education for southern black students was woefully underfunded. Washington and Rosenwald knew this and used their shared resources to build a total of "4,977 new schools, 217 teachers' homes, and 163 shops for the community's use." Construction costs totaled $28,408,520, which was quite a bit of money in those days and all days.

In the '70s, I found myself serving on the Tuskegee University Board of Trustees with William Rosenwald, the grandson of Julius Rosenwald. The Rosenwald family legacy of humanitarian philanthropy embodied the same values as the Good Samaritan who saved my father's life decades before.

I strongly believe that it is not religion or race that brings people together, but rather shared values. Booker T. Washington and Julius Rosenwald shared the same values. It didn't matter that one man was an African American protestant and the other was Jewish. They were both humanitarians, and together, they changed the world.

My mother attended a Rosenwald School near Miller's Ferry, Alabama, and that education equipped her to attend the Tuskegee Institute, where she trained to become a school teacher who would instruct and mentor many students, as well as all ten of her own children. In that way, the Tuskegee Circle had a positive impact on two generations of my family.

After graduating from the sixth grade, I moved on to Baldwin County Training School, where I attended seventh through twelfth grades.

The team of Rosenwald and Washington promoted visionary initiatives like the construction of Rosenwald Schools and the Tuskegee Institute, which ultimately became Tuskegee University in 1985.

Rosenwald's humanitarian efforts also reached out to educate farm families throughout the south, with community workshops to teach new and better agricultural practices.

Since my earliest years, Tuskegee University has been a positive influence in my life and has helped shape my social philosophy. Seeing the greatness of Booker T. Washington and Julius Rosenwald's work inspired me to extend educational lifelines to disadvantaged youth through my own philanthropic foundation. That became my passion and my most fulfilling endeavor.

It all began just before the turn of the century, in 1889, when the Eastern Shore Missionary Baptist Association purchased eighteen acres of land in Daphne, Alabama, to build a one-room private school. Baldwin County played host to the black Baptists who joined the movement to unify for the common cause of higher education in the region.

By 1916, after years of private operation and adding another building and several classrooms, the Eastern Shore Missionary Baptist Association deeded the school and eighteen acres to the state of Alabama. The school took on the new name of Eastern Shore Colored Industrial School. Later, it was renamed Baldwin County Training School.

I have always felt humbled when reflecting on the many educators who dedicated their lives to preparing students, including me, to go out into the world and make something of ourselves despite inadequate facilities and equipment.

White students received new books while we received their old markups—marked-up desks, furniture, and other discards. Even the buildings showed racial differentiation. White students learned in modern brick buildings while black schools were wood frame and, after years of deterioration, upgraded to cheap tile. White schools received complete football uniforms; black students were given work shoes with hard leather cleats for drilling into the ground.

Nevertheless, black students pushed ahead with zeal and determination. I can still hear W.J. Carroll, our principal, repeating his mantra: "You've got to get your lessons."

W.O. Jones, the agriculture and shop teacher, routinely reminded us to "Do the job, don't explain."

When a student asked what he meant, he answered, "When you do a job, you do it so well, it's self-explanatory." His eyes would blaze with zeal as he told us, "Without an education, you'll make a dollar an hour for the rest of your life."

Mr. Carroll and staff not only taught us from our books, but also they took personal responsibility to teach their students ethical and moral values for success:

- Be neat and clean and dress appropriately for any occasion.
- Be of high moral character.
- Be on time, every time.
- Your word is your bond.
- Have a good attitude toward yourselves and others.
- Be assertive, and when things get tough, get tougher.

We were taught to give direction to our lives by setting written goals and sticking to them but with the freedom to change if needed. Our teachers taught us about honesty and integrity, to treat others the way we wanted to be treated, to take pride in everything we did, and the desire to do everything as well as we could.

Baldwin County Training School teachers taught me to look for reasons to succeed rather than reasons to fail. We may have had substandard books and buildings, but our instructors taught us that success was not determined "by the cards you are dealt, but how well you play the game."

Our instructors didn't sugarcoat the fact that we were given less than white students. But they didn't bemoan it either. They showed us how to overcome despite the odds. Work shoes instead of cleats were not a reason to quit playing football. Old beat-up books were no reason not to study and cultivate our minds.

This culture of *positive possibilities* created a close bond with the students of Baldwin County Training School. We felt invested in the success of our school. If someone misbehaved, all the students would line up in two rows and pull off their belts, and the misbehaving student would run between the two rows while being whacked with our belts. No one was ever hurt, and all of us usually got a good laugh, even the ones who had misbehaved.

"Beltline" was indicative of the culture in our school—students kept each other in line. We all knew the consequences of division. Our path to success would be greatly hindered or impossible if we didn't work together. Misbehaving would invariably lead to a teacher-student-parent conference, and no one wanted to add fuel to the fire by complaining to parents about harsh treatment. Parents were mostly harsher than the teacher. And there was no tolerance in our village about misbehavior. You couldn't pay another student to keep your secret.

My family extended service and cooperation by storing, maintaining, and driving buses to and from Baldwin County Training School. First, my brother Joyful drove his younger siblings and students from the surrounding area to and from school every day. When Joyful went to college, my next oldest brother, Levaughn, drove the bus. I, in turn, drove the bus after him. It was our reasonable service. It was giving back.

The school owned the bus, but we parked, cleaned, and maintained it on our farm and drove the bus for only school transportation. Providing that transportation service for Baldwin County Training School students applied my values at home to those I learned at school, and those tasks cemented in me a lifelong commitment to community service.

In the aftermath of the US Supreme Court's ruling Brown versuss Board of Education and the subsequent social reforms brought on by the Civil Rights Movement, Baldwin County transitioned out of segregation and integrated its public schools between 1968 and 1972.

Local historian Harriet Outlaw says this transition went smoothly compared to other southern counties and credited that peaceful transition to the development of leadership in the black community. My brother Hilliard's two daughters were among the first students to integrate the schools.

Decades later, when the news reported that a move was underway to demolish the former Baldwin County Training School buildings, black, white, and other minority stakeholders formed the Baldwin County Training School Heritage Fest Foundation, which worked to preserve the history and values of our great teachers. It was my honor to contribute to that effort.

The year 2009 brought in the building that housed the home economics and agriculture classes, which officially converted to the Black Education Museum. I was honored to deliver the keynote address on July 1, 2009, at the grand opening of the new building.

In previous years, when I had been a student at Baldwin County Training School, I tried out for a public speaking contest. I practiced my speech to the cattle.

Hey, take any crowd you can find when you're just starting out.

Our community was a sterling example of the sort of village it takes to raise a child. My mother adopted Henrietta Jones, one of her former students, and raised her like one of her own daughters. That was the kind of love and warmth that permeated our village.

As I had prepared my keynote speech for the Black Education Museum, I realized how much Baldwin County and the rest of the nation had progressed in only three generations of the Jenkins' family line.

During my address, I expounded on how Abraham Lincoln signed the Emancipation Proclamation, freeing slaves in 1863 when blacks were not considered to be human beings. They were private property, bought and sold like any other commodity. It was against the law to educate them, and many lost their lives trying to elevate themselves by education.

Imagine losing your life just because you learned to read!

"Knowledge is power and education promotes liberty." That's how I ended that speech.

The genius of America is included in the Declaration of Independence and the US Constitution. Neither document was or ever will be perfect, but they offer a foundation by which citizens have the freedom to dissent, to push for justice and liberty. That's the reason Barack Obama was able, with hard work and determination, to become president of these United States.

No other country is like America, in spite of its imperfections. That's why it is incumbent upon each new generation to defend our rights—"to Life, Liberty and the pursuit of Happiness."

My parents and other great mentors in Alabama instilled in me that liberty and justice must first be defended in our families, our schools, and our communities. I still carry those principles securely inside of me. It is how I live my life.

> *We shall prosper as we learn to glorify and dignify labor and to put brains and skill into the common occupations of life.*

> —Booker T. Washington.

CHAPTER 8

❧❦❧

Tuskegee Ethos:
The Journey to Tuskegee

In late spring of 1951, a short time before graduating from Baldwin County Training School, my mother sat down in her rocking chair to have a talk with me. I positioned myself on the windowsill and listened.

"Son," she said, "you've got two choices to make now."

"What's that, Momma?" I asked.

"You can go to Tuskegee after you graduate high school next month, or you can leave home and make your own way in the world."

I was shocked that staying home and working on the farm was not an option. I felt like crying, like I was being booted out of my safety zone. I was being asked to leave home, family, and farm—all that I knew. I was content working on the family farm. I loved farming.

My mother eyed me as if she were waiting on me to decide right then and there. Her face was calm but stern.

I said nothing, only shrugged, and went outside for a while to think about things. I took a walk, and when I returned, I looked around the house and farm with fresh eyes. I loved it, but there was a great big world beyond its borders.

I was going to Tuskegee.

I wondered if my mother had that same talk with my five other sisters and brothers who had attended Tuskegee.

I didn't know the answer to that, but I was sure of one thing: my mother believed in the power of education, and she was guiding me to follow in her footsteps and those of my six older siblings. She knew from experience that Tuskegee would provide a safe and welcoming environment for my studies, just as it had for her older children. One of the many benefits Tuskegee offered—a solid education for upward mobility.

Had my mother not pushed me to attend that college, I might not have earned a college degree. I might not have traveled around the world. I wouldn't have met my wife.

That's the power parents have in pushing their children toward a good life—to broaden them to dream and think bigger than they otherwise would.

I asked my older brothers Joyful and Levaughn to tell me the toughest degree they offered at Tuskegee.

"Veterinary medicine," they said in unison.

"Huge workload, surprise tests, and hard grading curve," Joyful said. "It drives some of the students crazy."

"A whole lot drop out or transfer to easier majors," Levaughn laughed.

Right there on the spot, I said, "I'll take it."

Veterinary medicine was going to be my major. The thought of how hard it was only doubled my resolve to succeed.

Before facing the academic challenges in Veterinary medicine, I first had to get a job at Tuskegee to pay for food and board. I needed to prove in my first two years of pre-veterinary study that I was academically qualified to enter the formal veterinary program.

To get to Tuskegee, Levaughn, Connie, and I had big trunks filled with our belongings. As we walked toward the truck, I took a good long look at the vast expanse of the only home I'd ever known—shocks of green and gold in the fields, impeccable fence lines, and the many new buildings we'd constructed over the years. That view filled me with overwhelming pride and sadness all at the same time.

I loaded one of our family trucks, hugged my mom goodbye, and jumped in the open back with Levaughn and Connie. Joyful throttled the motor, and we were off to Tuskegee.

As the truck rumbled down Highway 80, I stared up at that big blue Alabama sky and thought about so many unknown challenges I'd face. I had no idea how useful the work ethic and values that had been instilled in me would prove beneficial in my future.

My mother repeated her advice over and over from the time I was very young, and it all came rushing back to me on the way to Tuskegee:

"Always carry yourself in a dignified manner, Matthew. Be strong, Matthew. Walk like you're going someplace, Matthew. Roll your shoulders back and walk with purpose, Matthew. Hold your head high, Matthew. Integrity is your spirit, Matthew."

She taught me to look a person in the eye and offer a confident handshake—to act like I *was* somebody if I wanted to *be* somebody. I can still feel the sensation of rolling my shoulders back, putting chest out, and raising my chin, walking with pride and presenting myself well. It seemed insignificant and routine back then, but now it felt empowering, monumental.

I could take on Tuskegee.

"Every man and woman cuts some kind of figure during a lifetime, Matthew. It's more important to cut a good figure than to buy cars or clothes."

"Yes, ma'am."

"What kind of figure do you want to cut in the world, Matthew?"

"A great one."

Some people need to serve in the military to learn discipline, but the Jenkins children got their discipline on the farm. I rose before sunrise, made my bed, dressed myself, and went to work with a focus on doing a good job. Those habits instilled in me the confidence that I could make it at Tuskegee because the cultural climate at home and at school were much the same. This was all summed up in a quote engraved on the Booker Washington monument at Tuskegee: "We shall prosper as we learn to glorify and dignify labor and to put brains and skill into the common occupations of life."

Washington demonstrated the merit of this view early in his career, long before he founded Tuskegee Institute, and even before he had a formal education. In his book, *Up from Slavery*, Washington recounts how, immediately after reaching the Hampton Institute campus, he "presented himself before the head teacher for assignment to a class."

Washington admitted that the long journey, lack of food, worn clothes, and his need for a bath must have been what caused the head teacher to look him up and down as if he were a worthless tramp, while admitting other students to class.

After twittering his fingers, reading, sleeping, and fidgeting, he got his chance. "Ma'am, if you'd like me to do anything while I wait, you just have to ask," he said.

She ignored him for three hours, maybe feeling that he would leave. He sat there looking in her direction, waiting for her instructions. After three hours, the head teacher acknowledged the gangly, country-looking young man was human and gave him what he'd asked for.

"See that broom?" She nodded toward the broom rack. "Take it and sweep the floor of the reception hall over there."

Washington sprang up and proceeded to sweep the floors three times, reaching under all the furniture. Then he took a cloth and dusted the corners four times. He pushed every piece of furniture away from the walls and dusted them.

When the head teacher went over to check on her ward, she couldn't believe her eyes. She took her handkerchief and wiped the surfaces, counters, shelves, floorboards, and other less obvious places. The handkerchief was still clean.

"I guess you'll get into Hampton after all," she said.

Washington went on to become the founding president of the Tuskegee Institute. From that story, I learned that one should never be too prideful to do whatever needs to be done. Most successful people take pride in everything they do—if you're going to do something, do it right, every time. Every obstacle is just a step on the way to success. I concluded that an exemplary life is built with step-by-step diligence.

Washington's life, to me, was a case study in step-by-step diligence and perseverance. Since he had only fifty cents to his name
when he arrived at Hampton Institute, he took a job as a janitor to
pay for his room and board.

Imagine going to class and then sweeping up after the class was
over!

"I was determined from the first to make my work as janitor
so valuable that my services would be indispensable," Washington
wrote, adding, "I succeeded in doing my job so well that the school
soon informed me that the full cost of my board had been paid."

But Washington faced an even bigger challenge: the seven-
ty-dollar-a-year tuition fee.

"If I had been compelled to pay the tuition, in addition to my
board, I would have been compelled to leave Hampton Institute,"
Washington acknowledged.

Fortunately, General Samuel C. Armstrong, the founder and
first principal of the Hampton Institute, noticed Washington's exemplary diligence and persuaded a wealthy northern donor to pay for his
education. Washington described General Armstrong as "the noblest,
rarest human being that had ever been my privilege to meet." He
became General Armstrong's most famous protégé.

Armstrong and Washington shared a profound love and respect
for each other, a relationship built upon shared humanitarian values.
"I have spoken of my admiration for General Armstrong, and yet he
was but a type of that Christlike body of men and women who went
into the Negro schools during the Civil War to assist in lifting up my
race."

I was beginning to deepen my appreciation of such dignified
and noble souls, united by common values to help others, and ready
to dismiss divisive issues of race, class, and religion, and instead pursue a higher humanitarian calling. Those men were like the Good
Samaritan who nursed my father back to health after he was beaten by
the KKK. Such a man was Julius Rosenwald, who donated millions
of dollars to educate rural blacks, not because they shared the same
race or religion, but because they held the same values as Washington
and General Armstrong.

And now me.

Washington observed how Armstrong was never bitter toward southern whites even though he fought against them during the Civil War. Rather, Armstrong "was constantly seeking to find ways by which he could be of service to southern whites." In this way, Armstrong, a white general, shared the same values as my African American parents, who taught their children to reject all forms of hate and bitterness.

One of the greatest discoveries during my lifetime was that the values passed down to me from my ancestors—the blood relations I call the Lost Tribe—connected me to humanitarians of every race, religion, and gender.

In the beginning, humans were all one tribe. Over the centuries, racial, religious, class, political, and countless other divisive customs and traditions have brought about the most repugnant human rights atrocities, dividing the spirit of the original tribe and tragically estranging us from one another, sapping all their essential humanity.

In the face of this age-old struggle, people from every corner of the world and throughout history have rejected inhumane habits in order to embrace humanitarian deeds.

What happened to the Lost Tribe?

I meant that in terms of my kin, but as the years passed and I learned more about the great men and women who lived before me, I began to view the Lost Tribe through a more inclusive lens, one that embraces any person who shares the values of my tribe.

Every Good Samaritan throughout history is part of this larger continuum of humanitarianism—the people who share their successes with others in need, the people who regard every man and woman as their equal, and the people who do unto others as they would have done unto them.

If you don't believe in the wisdom in Washington's views on work ethic, consider this alternative story.

There was a builder who worked for the same housing developer for many years. One day, the developer told the builder, "This is the last house we're going to build."

The builder felt resentful that his job was coming to an end and he allowed that one incident to corrupt his work ethic. Instead of using two-by-six boards, he used two-by-fours. He used low-grade glass instead of double-pane glass for the windows. He cut corners at every turn and used inferior materials.

When construction was finished, the developer said to the contractor, "You know, you've worked for me for many years, so I'm going to give you a present." He handed the builder a set of keys. "I'm giving this last house to you."

People who do shoddy work ruin their reputation. You might get away with it here and there, but one day, it will show up in the light, pointing to its maker.

Booker T. Washington summed it up this way: "Those people who 'glorify and dignify labor' by putting their 'brains and skill into' each and every action will develop a reputation that will open many other doors of opportunity."

I believe that too.

In the end, your reputation is all you have. If you tarnish it, doors of opportunity will slam shut. So my advice to any youngster is this: "Don't half do anything. To see a botched job appalls me. If you can't do it right, keep trying until you get there. If you're really stumped, ask for help from someone you respect." We all need mentors who inspire us to live our best lives. My most important mentor at Tuskegee was Dr. Frederick Douglass Patterson, president of Tuskegee Institute and founder of The United Negro College Fund. Dr. Patterson would have a profound influence on my life.

CHAPTER 9

❦

Morning Walks with Dr. Patterson

During my first two years at the Tuskegee Institute, I followed in the footsteps of my brothers Levaughn and Joyful. They worked for Dr. Irving A. Derbigny, vice president of Tuskegee. Just like the positive reputation that Levaughn and Joyful established when they drove buses to and from Baldwin County Training School, their excellent work ethic put me next in line to work for Dr. Derbigny, and he gladly hired another Jenkins.

A positive reputation opens doors.

As Dr. Derbigny's personal assistant, I drove him to and from the airport and maintained his house and grounds. Like most of the leadership at the Tuskegee Institute, he was humble and personable. He would ask how I was doing in school, how my mother was faring, and if I was happy. I admired him more than I can say.

Later in life, as a business owner, I sought to maintain such cordial relationships with my employees, no matter their level of experience. I found that something as simple as asking about their well-being or a Christmas bonus would foster loyalty and care for the business.

My life changed dramatically during my first year at Tuskegee, but one thing didn't change—my love for getting up early in the morning. Before work and just after sunrise, I enjoyed taking morning walks around campus. It turned out that Dr. Patterson, the president of Tuskegee Institute, also took morning walks around campus about the same time. That's how I met my mentor, a man who would influence my life in a positive way for decades.

I never formally asked Dr. Patterson to be my mentor; it just happened. When we'd take our morning walks and would run into each other, we'd walk together. I was honored to have those morning walks and talks with Dr. Patterson.

He had been directly responsible for bringing both military aviation and veterinary medicine to Tuskegee, and that impacted my aspirations for veterinary medicine and my brothers to pursue aviation. I felt comfortable enough to discuss anything with Dr. Patterson.

As a veterinarian himself, he understood the difficult nature of my curriculum, and beyond the books, he understood the hands-on nature of pulling a calf or conducting in-depth surgery. In short, he was a wealth of knowledge and experience, and he generously shared both with me. He never called me by name. To Dr. Patterson, I was always "Young Man."

"Young Man," he said to me one morning, "you're going to be very wealthy one day. And when you are, I want you to remember to help those less fortunate than you."

I had always been a bit puzzled by how much time and resources my mother gave to others in need, and he had just given me the key to our family's survival and success after my father's sudden death. Giving was the key.

"Mom, why do you do all this for other people?" I had asked.

"One day, you'll understand."

Dr. Patterson brought me to the very core of that understanding. His wisdom agreed with the foundational values I learned from my family. His influence prepared my commitment for helping others, doing community service, and leaving a legacy.

Dr. Patterson compelled me to ask myself tough questions: *What is my purpose? What contribution am I to make?*

In the interim, I learned that a person's purpose is to contribute something worthwhile to the world. Each person has an obligation to do that. No one was born to live selfishly. Man is meant to make life better.

Greedy and selfish people are empty vessels. Their greed and self-indulgence never add much to life.

I thanked my mother and Dr. Patterson for teaching me that the real test of success is how you share what you have with others—be it wisdom, knowledge, experience, or material things.

In all my business and political dealings, in all my travels, I've found that common values bring people together. I carried the values I learned at home to college, and there I met a wise mentor who shared the same values that strengthened my own. That is the power of instilling wholesome, humanitarian values in children. When they leave home, they seek out those same values in mentors, friends, and mates.

It chills me to think of the opposite scenarios—when parents instill greed and hatred in their children. When those children leave the nest, far too many fly in troubled skies. The culture at the Tuskegee Institute guided me to bright skies, rich with opportunity.

During those morning walks, Dr. Patterson would say, "You know, I wish there were ways to provide more opportunities for these black kids who don't have a way to go to college."

Only a man as humble as Dr. Patterson would say such a thing, given his experience. In 1944, he founded the United Negro College Fund, a philanthropic organization that provided operating funds for thirty-eight historically black colleges and universities. It also provided scholarships and internships for students, along with professional training for faculty and administrative staff.

The organization has raised more than forty billion dollars for disadvantaged students to attend colleges and universities, especially those living in rural and southern areas. UNCF distributes more funds to help minorities attend school than any organization outside of the US government.

I was impressed that Dr. Patterson was responsible for founding the most important philanthropic organization for disadvantaged minorities seeking a college education and yet still was not satisfied. I admired him in the same way I admired Booker T. Washington. Both men understood that education was the great equalizer.

Washington was not satisfied with the institute's single building and one hundred acres. Rather than falling into complacency, he brought together a broad coalition of supporters to raise expansion funds. From that bold innovation, Tuskegee University increased its land holdings to five thousand acres and more than a hundred buildings.

I came to understand the common thread joining those two giants. Both Washington and Patterson were never satisfied with the status quo. They knew that for every minority student getting an education, there were thousands who were not, and we understood that building loyal coalitions of supporters with humanitarian values was the key to survival and expansion. Those lessons proved invaluable when my wife and I founded our philanthropic organization— The Matthew and Roberta Jenkins Family Foundation. Even in that effort, Dr. Patterson was my trusted mentor.

My feelings for Dr. Patterson mirror the deep love and admiration Booker T. Washington expressed for his mentor, General Armstrong. It didn't matter a bit that Armstrong was white and Washington was black. Leaders like Armstrong, Washington, Rosenwald, and Patterson shared the same humanitarian values. They understood that knowledge is power and people deprived of basic education are subject to lower productivity and mistreatment by others.

The day after the passage of the Emancipation Proclamation, freed slaves faced the monumental challenge of obtaining an education that had been withheld from them and their ancestors for centuries. I can't emphasize enough how important the efforts of leaders like Armstrong, Washington, Rosenwald, and Patterson were in helping black Americans access education, work, and dignity.

One progressive plan that Dr. Patterson introduced was what is now known as the "Five-Year Plan." When he assumed the presidency, Tuskegee Institute was running a deficit. To address this, he carefully reviewed all institute costs and found that many support staff positions were held by employees without degrees, in some cases, not even high school diplomas. Most received wages nearly commensurate with MA and MS degree holders.

Dr. Patterson used the imbalance and related deficit challenge as an opportunity to innovate. He eliminated the overpaid support positions and directed his staff to place advertisements around the country for any student with a *B* average or better who was unable to finance a college education. He offered those students the opportunity to matriculate from Tuskegee Institute and earn a four-year degree in five years without incurring any debt whatsoever. In return, the student agreed to work during the day and take a half day's academic program at night for two years.

Dr. Patterson wrote in his autobiography: "They would then have achieved freshman year. We agreed to pay them $1,200 for services rendered rather than in cash. Their earnings became a book entry on which they could draw with a part-time job during the next three years while attending school full time."

CHRONICLES
OF FAITH

The Autobiography of
Frederick D. Patterson

Edited by Martia Graham Goodson

With a Foreword by Harry V. Richardson

The genius of the Five-Year Plan was that it gave students vital professionalization by establishing a work ethic, time management, and a sound understanding of professional attire and conduct. Initially, students would work "a full day under their instructors until they were proficient and grow to become worth the wages they were paid. Then when they transitioned to part-time jobs for three years, they were skilled workers rather than inexperienced novices."

I was a sponge in the hands of this great mentor. Dr. Patterson devised a brilliant game plan to address two separate challenges: to help more disadvantaged youth earn college degrees, while turning a $150,000 deficit into a surplus of $300,000. He demonstrated that humanitarianism and philanthropy can work hand in hand profitably.

For many students who came to Tuskegee with little more than the shirt on their back, the Five-Year Plan gave them the chance to earn an otherwise unobtainable education. Graduates of the Five-Year Plan went on to successful careers as lawyers, doctors, and officers and generals in the US military among other professions.

I share Dr. Patterson's view that the Five-Year Plan should never have been retired. Moreover, I feel the Five-Year Plan offered a template that educators can still use to address the skyrocketing costs of education in the twenty-first century.

On June 23, 1987, President Ronald Reagan awarded Dr. Patterson the Presidential Medal of Freedom, the highest honor a United States citizen can receive. I was thrilled that my mentor, a man of almost frustrating humility, finally earned the recognition he so deserved. I could not think of a better mentor than Dr. Patterson. He always told me that if I dreamed big, I would enjoy great success with which to share with the world.

And so I have.

CHAPTER 10

⟶⬥⟵

Cultivating a Surgeon's Precision

I completed my second year of nonclinical study with strong grades, which granted me formal admittance into the School of Veterinary Medicine at Tuskegee Institute. With my pre-vet requirements completed, I began lab and clinical work, which proved to be invaluable experience for my future veterinary career.

Because of the rigors of the program, all students studying veterinary medicine were eligible to live in Phelps Hall, a dorm devoted to our field and master's degree students. Phelps Hall afforded me a peaceful place to sleep and study. I believe school administrators were wise to give veterinary and masters students a dorm where we did not have to deal with the typical college shenanigans, because none of us could afford to miss a single night of study. Our future depended upon preparation. The work ethic I cultivated on the family farm prepared me for the rigorous study necessary to excel in veterinary medicine.

In my fifth year, I found that I could live rent free if I assisted the clinicians with cleaning the test tubes and equipment in the parasitology lab and accompany clinicians when they went on large animal calls. I took the job. I went to work at 3:00 a.m. Being the only one in the lab, I bought a used radio for eight dollars to keep me company. After my morning lab work, I ate breakfast and went to class.

What an honor it was to graduate from Tuskegee with honors! Benjamin Franklin's "Early to bed, early to rise, makes a man healthy, wealthy, and wise" proved to be very true in my case. A common trait in many successful people is that they are in the habit of rising early. I've done it my whole life. I've always looked forward to the next morning—the little streak of sunrise would tell me it was time I hit the floor. I've never used an alarm clock, even during veterinary school. You can train your mind to wake up on time. And yes, that habit delivered to me the most difficult degree Tuskegee offered.

I think it all started with Dr. Miller, our family veterinarian. Whenever he visited our farm to check our animals, I'd assist him. He told me about earning his degree from Auburn University while he administered tests and shots. I carefully watched the techniques he used to pull calves and treat hogs. He became my first veterinary role model.

From those early days, I learned the routine of milking cows and tending to baby bulls and other farm animals. From that childhood experience, I was at ease with most any animal, including cats and dogs. I believe part of the reason I was always relaxed and composed during my professional years of surgical operations is because I had dewormed and castrated our cattle and hogs on the farm since I was a boy.

I had also cleaned more rabbits, birds, and squirrels than I could count. My older brothers loved to hunt small game. Sometimes, they'd bring home dozens of squirrels and rabbits, and I was delegated to clean all them. I didn't mind. I could clean them better than anyone in the family anyway, so I was happy to do it. It was the same as when I got excited about plowing the fields. I enjoyed the act of precision these tasks required.

Recently, my brother Samuel came to visit me in Long Beach, and while sitting on the patio enjoying the cool ocean breeze, I thought of life on the farm. I asked Samuel why he and the others always wanted me to be the first to plow the crops.

"You did it better than anybody else," he answered. "You were meticulous. You knew how to set the plows just right, and you'd always plow straight down the row. Even when you were nine or ten, we'd just leave you on your own. We never had to redo any of your work."

That felt good to hear, even after all the time that had passed.

A field is plowed a number of times, but any farmer worth his salt knew that the first plow was the most important. That first plow occurred just after the corn and beans would sprout. A botched first plow would cover the baby plants in dirt and ruin the entire crop. Precision is imperative. All the later plows and harvesting depended upon that first plow. A good first plow was like a healthy mental habit: each subsequent effort becomes easier. A successful first plow established trenches that the next worker could follow straight down the line. It took precision to reap the abundant crops we needed for a successful season.

During my studies, I overdosed myself on veterinary medicine. I became proficient in a wide range of surgeries and other procedures, and my confidence grew.

I had done an internship in New York and was moving steadily toward my profession. I was there two weeks and literally ran the place by the time I left. I did most of the surgeries as well as cleaning cages and scrubbing floors. After that summer, I returned from New York thinking I was a hot shot. A New York newspaper even published a story about my abilities.

When I was back in Alabama, my sister Connie asked me to do her a favor. "Matt, can you spay Jackie for me?"

That brought me right back down to earth. I was a big shot, and someone was asking me to fix their dog. *That's the life!*

I ate some pot roast, boiled corn, and greens in the school cafeteria, which reminded me of my mother's meals. Then I washed my hands like a vet, put on my white surgical shirt, and rolled up my sleeves, all prepped to spay my sister's boxer.

I cut the tail and ears in the stand-up form common to boxers. She looked like a show dog. Connie was going to be happy. I disinfected her, made sure of where to make the incisions, and spayed her.

But Jackie wasn't recovering like I expected. I gave her some stimulants to wake her up, but her breathing became shallow. Jackie then took a single deep breath and opened her eyes only slightly, and her head slumped to the side. I threw my head back in complete devastation.

I had killed my sister's dog.

I wanted to cry. I loved that dog as much as Connie did. I always hated to lose any animals in my care—but this one was special—she was Connie's. I needed a right-now plan.

Somehow, some of the students leaked it to the dean of the School of Veterinary Medicine, and they ribbed me for it the entire day. Worst of all, I had to face Connie. I took a giant step to make the best of a bad situation. I accepted what I had done. I could neither deny nor ignore that I had failed to perform a successful surgery on my sister's dog.

I called Connie and told her straight out what had happened. I considered that my sister might hate me forever, but I had to tell her and grieve with her for a while, and that's exactly what I did.

By the next day, my private tragedy turned into public teasing, which forced me to confront my experience and renew my determination to become an excellent doctor. I had done too much surgery on Jackie. Being young and inexperienced, I'd moved too rapidly to do the surgeries because I had done a lot of them in my training. But I learned that operating like a good professional requires clear and deliberate judgment.

Success is all about learning from failure. Failure is the opportunity to learn.

When you fail, there's room to improve. I knew then and there that there is no defeat, only setbacks on the way to success. Success is a long process of many steps forward, not a fleeting, final event.

As any surgeon knows, sometimes, perfectly conducted procedures do not yield successful results. Even more sobering was that the world's best surgeons lose patients. Accepting and learning that truth from a lost dog helped me to establish my professional modus operandi. I put the tragedy behind me and found myself in a constant quest for *positive possibilities*.

If finding *positive possibilities* in failure seems difficult, consider this notion: if you are wrong seventy percent of the time in Major League Baseball, you are batting three hundred and on your way to an all-star career. It's not uncommon for batters to hit home runs after a series of strikeouts.

Finding the positive in losing that dog made me a better surgeon. It also built upon the wisdom passed down to me: *Refuse to let your mind get bogged down with negatives you can't control.* After that experience, the more I practiced, the easier the task became.

That is an approach I've used in every aspect of my life. Eventually, I learned to turn on a dime. I learned to keep my mind fresh by discovering progressive things to improve my life and that of those around me. Some student might have become gun-shy and not gone into practice if they lost an animal like I did, but to me, it was a tremendous challenge. And I've always liked challenges.

After I received my doctorate and started my practice, I went to UCLA and took courses in surgery, and that extra study allowed me to operate at the top of my game.

Sacrifice = Success

First Generation Game Plan

I learned early in life that goals are useless without a game plan to reach them. I learned that goals need daily implementation and reflection. My mom's training, coupled with Dr. Patterson's moral and ethical guidance, made it crystal clear to me that success was more than financial wealth.

True success means enriching the lives of others to make the world a better place for all. True success means fulfilling one's purpose in life, even if it means struggling to fulfill difficult goals. Inheriting large sums of money does not mean you're successful; it just means you've become financially wealthy. It means you can buy things that are not necessarily beneficial to anyone. If you don't believe that, look at those lottery winners who tangle themselves in more problems than they had before winning the jackpot!

In my freshman year, I set my life goals. I had learned the value of writing down specific long-term goals and then breaking them into a series of short-term actions. One goal was to start my own veterinary practice after graduating and fulfilling my military requirements. I planned to work seven days a week for seven years to build my practice and reach profitability. I planned to invest in real estate. I planned to find a mate.

The woman I married would be a critical part of my success. She would need to share my values and be supportive of the sacrifices we made together to fulfill our goals.

While in college, I felt that the right woman for me would understand the time I spent in my quest for academic excellence. I would allow nothing to interfere with my education. More than once, I had to tell some girl I was dating that education was my top priority. I had to decline social events to meet my academic goals.

My limited social life frustrated the girls who didn't share my values. I'd tell them, "If you see somebody out there you like, don't let me hold you back. I can't fall behind in my education."

Many weekends, when friends would invite me to parties or beer blasts, I'd say, "I've got to study."

The School of Veterinary Medicine at Tuskegee was still in its infancy when I was in college. It was the first black school in the United States teaching veterinary medicine. Dr. Patterson, a veterinarian himself, set the bar very high because he and other school leaders wanted to graduate the best students. That way, young Tuskegee alums would be able to compete in a prejudiced society, because discriminatory laws made it more difficult for black veterinarians to compete with their white counterparts. Later in my career, I helped to eliminate many of those discriminatory laws.

To make an *A* grade in my program, you needed to score ninety-four percent and above, a grade of *B* required eighty-six to ninety-three percent, and a *C* required seventy-seven to eighty-five percent. Seventy to seventy-six percent got you a *D*. And those high standards of academia brought several unannounced exams with them too.

I studied every night for the next day. I stayed disciplined.

Studying veterinary medicine taught me that the most difficult tasks could be accomplished by consistently taking small steps. I focused on the task with tenacity and no distractions. Even now, half a century later, I turn off the television when I'm reading because I want to gain insight into my main focus, with nothing to distract me from my goal.

Sacrifice means refusing to indulge in short-term trifles and meaningless gratification when a vitally important task is at hand. Earned success is all about sacrifice. Those studying medicine, law, or engineering, athletes aspiring to the Olympics, and entrepreneurs seeking to build national and global businesses, are all examples of people who share a common practice on the road to success—sacrifice!

CHAPTER 11

❦

Head and Heart in Unison

From an early age, I expected to work twice as hard as the next person to reach my goals. I expected sacrifice. Surprisingly, my most challenging test would be finding a beautiful woman who embodied my common values and goals.

While growing up, all my sisters and brothers knew my mother loved and respected my father and that he loved and respected her. My mother's training and values became a moral compass that would guide me in times of uncertainty. She emphasized how important it was to look for certain qualities and values in the woman I would marry. So I wanted someone who was educated, who had high moral values, a respect for family, and who was capable of working with me. I've had friends tell me how their spouses are not supportive of their goals and values.

"Man!" one of my friends once said. "My wife doesn't do anything!"

Their marriage ended in divorce. I've had many friends in similar situations, and none of them grew or prospered. I believe it's safe to say that if you and your spouse's life goals and values are not in harmony, the discord can wreak havoc. And harmony is never easy.

After more than fifty years of marriage, I'm more certain than ever that our shared values made for a good marriage. My wife and I came from the same culture of hard work, honesty, high expectations, drive, and determination. So when we got together, our hearts and minds were in harmony. In this new century, it's like we're still newlyweds. Her family is my family. We've never had a major conflict. In fact, her siblings say that if they had to choose between the two of us, they'd have to think long and hard on that decision!

Her family and I get along just great, which includes lots of laughs. But to become one with this great woman and her family, I made major decisions early in my life.

Yogi Berra says it this way: "When you reach a fork in the road, take it."

Like all Yogi's famous lines, that makes for great comedy; but in reality, we all must make clear decisions. We must choose paths that require sacrifice—closing one door to open another. The toughest decisions are most often tangled with deep emotions.

Long before I met my wife, the steps to a harmonious marriage were not yet clear, but they were certainly important. By 1956, I could breathe a bit from my studies, and I started looking towards the future. In my sophomore year, I started dating a girl I was crazy about. I called her "Heat Wave," because every time she was near, I felt my body heating up. But deep down, I sensed she wasn't right for me. I tried to rationalize her as a potential mate, but I'd always end up reaching the same conclusion: *I love that girl with my heart, but my head tells me no. It's not going to be good for either of us.*

Those Sunday morning breakfast talks my mother used to have with us about choosing a good mate always came to mind when I'd see my girlfriend because I was so crazy about her. But as enamored as I was, I couldn't deny the signals. There was no giant red flag, just the appearance of different values.

I observed her habits, her work ethic, and her questionable career choice. It was vexing for me to experience this tug-of-war between intuition and desire. I couldn't escape the feeling that something between us didn't quite fit. They were little things that I knew would eventually lead to conflict. I was prepared to sacrifice and do whatever was required to support a family, and I wanted a wife who would tie our family values together as one and be a good mother for our kids.

I wanted to marry someone who would be joined at my hip, moving forward as one strong unit. Those qualities were missing in that college romance.

I wanted to go to the top of whatever mountains I found in my path, and I knew I couldn't climb that height if I had to carry the weight of a bad marriage. So I determined my goal and set my game plan to reach the top, which meant I had no choice but to end that relationship. I also knew it would be very difficult for me to resist the heat wave in the future. Never before had I felt so vulnerable in the presence of my desires.

I wrote a note to myself:

Whenever you see her, turn around and walk the other way.

I placed that note on the mirror in my room so that I saw it every morning. That was step one for reaching my goal. Step two was more difficult—implementing my game plan. Every time I saw her on campus, I had to turn and go the other way. I knew that if I walked up to her, my desire could overwhelm my will. I understood my vulnerabilities.

I turned and walked the other way for six weeks before I could trust myself not to resume our romance. That experience helped me identify the tension between the head and the heart. The heart doesn't care about tomorrow or much of anything except feeling good in the moment. The head moves the mind, which helps us to implement our values and pursue our goals. Implementing my game plan required sacrifice, and a sacrifice of the heart usually does not feel good in the moment.

I had to take control.

CHAPTER 12

❖❖❖

My First Walk with Roberta

Finally, it was my last year in college, and prior to that year, I hadn't wanted a serious relationship with anybody until I was ready to graduate from veterinary school. I ended up bouncing around with a lot of girls and acquired the reputation of a playboy, but the truth was that I spent the lion's share of my time studying, not tomcatting. In fact, my true desire was to meet my soul mate.

I always figured I would know the right woman when I met her. In that respect, I was much like Martin Luther King. On his first date with Coretta Scott, Martin Luther King, Jr. said he knew he wanted to marry her because she had everything he ever wanted in a woman.

That's what I desired—character, intelligence, personality, and beauty. But the day of my graduation was drawing near, and I still hadn't met my wife to be. I didn't want to graduate from college without a potential wife in sight. I wanted somebody who would love me before I was a doctor, because after becoming a doctor, women come out of the woodwork.

But this Sunday afternoon, as I was taking a leisurely stroll across campus with no wife prospects in mind or in sight, I saw Roberta Jones descending a flight of stairs.

Let me tell you, that was a beautiful sight.

In her freshman year, I had noticed the beautiful new girl with the soft smile but rarely spoke to her. Occasionally, we passed each other going in opposite directions and exchanged casual greetings. She'd always acknowledge me with a cheerful smile.

"Hey, Jenkins!" she'd say, dashing off.

"Hi, Jones," I'd say, and off I'd go.

But this Sunday afternoon, there was no hustle and bustle. Just Roberta, descending the stairs, walking toward me, and I finally saw what I had missed seeing in her so many times before. Her smile was careful, and she dressed and carried herself with dignity. I was certain she came from a wholesome family.

"Where you off to?" I asked.

"To the movies," she answered.

The mile walk to the local theatre will give me time to get to know her. "Mind if I walk with you?" I asked.

"Sure." She shrugged.

With autumn leaves falling, we had a wonderful walk. I told her about the farm and my family; she told me about her family's dairy and her five sisters and one brother. Both of our families were farmers, so we laughed a lot about the chores we'd been assigned from an early age.

When we got back to campus, Roberta looked at me and smiled. "I had a whole different picture of you. I thought you were a playboy."

That was the moment I knew I had met the girl I could marry.

With her character, intelligence, personality, and beauty, I realized that she was the woman I could marry. It was a discovery that warmed my heart.

"Naught, I just had a lot of studying to do and didn't want to settle with one person then," I answered.

Her eyes searched my face with a bit of suspicion, but then she smiled again. After that first walk, Roberta and I started dating. I had a good feeling about her.

Whenever I was with her, I felt like my head and my heart were in unison. As our relationship grew, I became certain that Roberta was the woman I would marry. However, in a more sober mind-set, I took charge and set my game plan.

My days at Tuskegee were quickly drawing to a close. I planned to take a job in Massachusetts after graduating and then serve two years in the military to save enough money to launch my own veterinary practice. I had bold plans for my future, and I wanted to make that journey with Roberta. Three months later, as we walked across campus one afternoon, I stopped in the middle of the path.

"I want to meet your parents," I said.

"I've got a boyfriend back home."

"So?"

Roberta hadn't told me about an old high school sweetheart back home, and I had never seen him on campus. She had compartmentalized him until I raised the issue of visiting her family.

"Well," Roberta said, "you're making all these plans."

"I'm a planner. Stick with me, babe, and I'll take you places."

Like most serious things in my life, when it came to our relationship, I didn't mess around. I cut to the chase.

"When can I meet them?" I repeated.

"I'll let you know next week," she said cautiously.

The following week, Roberta told me she had called her mother and asked if she could bring me home to meet the family, and the next weekend, we took a bus to Augusta, Georgia. Her mother picked us up at the bus station. I saw where Roberta had gotten her good looks. Her mother was a knockout.

As we entered Roberta's home, I felt at ease. Her parents were friendly, and docile Jersey cattle were grazing in the fields outside.

That evening, Roberta's father gave me a tour of the dairy barn. I watched how the workers washed the udders on the Jersey cows before attaching the milking tools. I observed the pasteurizing and bottling facilities.

Roberta's father Sam told me that his team of drivers loaded the milk on trucks before sunrise and delivered bottles to customers and stores throughout the county.

Her father and I hit it off immediately. He had the same entrepreneurial spirit as my own father.

By dinnertime, I had met Roberta's five sisters and a brother, all smiling and friendly, and I felt completely welcome. Roberta's family fell in love with me and I with them. She and I were being joined together with good common values and hospitality.

I didn't try to impress Roberta's family. Our positive interaction was a product of our shared values and teachings. I was taught that whenever you go to visit a person in their home, you connect with them on their turf and terms. If they're digging potatoes, you dig potatoes. If they're cutting grass, you cut grass too. If they're sweeping floors, grab a broom and sweep. As I followed my training at her home, our love and relationship were sealed.

Some call "hearth" the center of a family home. For me and my family, it was the dining room table, and I was completely at ease sitting around the Jones's dinner table with Roberta and her family. It was clear that she and I were compatible, through and through.

Finally, after dinner, we were alone, sitting in a swing in the darkness of her porch. Crickets chirped and lightning bugs twinkled around the redwood swing on the north end of the porch. All around the white picket fence was total blackness. I was amazed at how much our families were alike.

"Where did your mother grow up?" I asked.

"She was born on a plantation in Beech Island, South Carolina."

"Must be a story behind that."

"Yeah, and you don't want to hear it," she answered.

"Ah, come on." I coaxed.

I could see her silhouette in the darkness. She looked straight ahead, as if she were about to say something she didn't want to share. She hesitated and then began her story.

"My great-grandfather on my mother's side was Alfred Hammond, the grandson of James Hammond, governor and senator of South Carolina. Senator-Governor James Hammond was well known for his staunch support of slavery. Now think about that."

She kept looking straight ahead instead of turning to look at me. Her pace picked up. "My great-grandmother Annie worked as a cook and housekeeper on the family plantation most of her life. She had three children by Alfred Hammond—Sadie, Carrie, and Cecil. In those days, even though slavery was over, the culture remained the same. Many former slaves worked for the same people who had owned them.

"When I was old enough to discover some of the family secrets, it became apparent that my great-grandmother, Mamma Annie, had been a slave, where people were bought and sold like cattle on our dairy farm."

I listened in rapt silence as she told her story.

"In Mamma Annie's older years, after she retired from the plantation, she came to live with our family. She fell in love with my baby sister, Mary, and spent much of her time telling us tales of her past. While we enjoyed her stories, our favorite time with her was when she sat on the steps in her lilac dress and allowed us to comb and braid her silky blonde hair."

"That's kind of a familiar story," I said, trying to ease the pain I heard in her voice. Roberta didn't respond but kept talking. I felt protective of her, sitting so close to me, sharing her innermost thoughts. I felt something for her I had never felt for any other girl.

"It's our history till we change it," I whispered, knowing that things ran deeper than history with Roberta in that moment. It seemed as though she needed to show that she trusted me with her pain.

"When I'd ask my mother about the stories I'd heard and other odd things I'd learned about our family, she'd say, 'I don't know.' At other times, she'd start to cry." At that point, Roberta started to swing again.

"My grandmother Carrie died when my mother was ten. My mother was called Little Sadie. My mother's aunt, called Big Sadie, moved my mom and her brother Mont to Augusta, Georgia, with her. Big Sadie became the only grandmother I knew on my mother's side of the family.

"Big Sadie had grown up working as household help for the Hammond family. She bore the Hammond name but was treated like a servant." Roberta paused, as if understanding the depth of that injustice for the first time.

"One fall day when I was a young woman, I attended Big Sadie's funeral. And it all made complete sense to me. As I stood by her grave, I saw two white women huddled near me, talking in low voices.

"'Sadie was our blood cousin,' one of them said.

"'I know,' the other woman answered.

"And that was the end of Big Sadie to them. It was that dismissive sum total of her life for all the years of faithful service she'd given the Hammond family. She was never acknowledged as a human being, a good worker, or their kin, until after she'd passed."

I was silent. Roberta's story reminded me of the one my family told me about the Ku Klux Klan beating my father nearly to death. Our mutual pain bonded us together.

❖

The following month, I took Roberta to Baldwin County to meet my family. Taking your sweetheart home to meet your family can be a nerve-racking experience, but I was relatively calm, because by then, I felt assured that our destiny as man and wife was a foregone conclusion. I was not surprised when my mother and siblings received Roberta as warmly as her parents and six siblings had received me.

On April 20, 1958, we were married in Bath, South Carolina. Roberta and I were compatible to a tee. Standing in the church with Roberta at my side, I thought how fortunate I was to have found a kindred spirit. Our culture of self-reliance, entrepreneurialism, and pragmatic goal setting unified us even more than the words of the old Baptist minister.

"I now pronounce you man and wife." I kissed the bride.

As we walked out, I stopped and lifted Roberta's chin and kissed her again, thinking she was absolutely the most perfect mate I could have ever hoped to find. We were perfect partners from day one, soul mates now for more than fifty years.

Looking back, it still amazes me how casually some men choose a life partner. They deliberate over where to go on vacation, when buying a house or a computer, but their wives are chosen by emotion.

To me, choosing a mate was one of the most important decisions of my life, and I believed that deeply enough to make sure we were right for each other, even after my heart told me she was the woman for me.

I've seen too many people get divorced because they allowed their heart to dominate their head. Life is all about balance, and the decisions we make that affect us for a lifetime must be considered with tender loving care.

I'm proud to have chosen my mate with a balance between my head and my heart. I knew all those years ago with Roberta, that we would have the peace and camaraderie to focus on our future together, and we would never part.

And after fifty years, we never have.

CHAPTER 13

The Draft Board

I registered for the draft when I turned eighteen. It was my duty to my country. I planned on serving two years in the air force after earning my doctorate. I knew that work would be scarce after graduation, but I wanted to secure work, serve my country, and save money to open a veterinary practice.

The draft board had other plans.

In early 1957, before I graduated from Tuskegee, I learned that the local Alabama Draft Board was trying to draft me as a private before I earned the doctorate degree of veterinary medicine, a degree that would give me officer status. If the military drafted me before graduation, I would have to enter as a private, and I would also be denied the time I needed to earn a DVM degree.

Legally, I should have been exempt from the draft until graduation, but institutional racism in the military, attitudes, and policies of the draft board threatened my academic and career aspirations.

I had two options: I could be angry or apathetic, or I could adjust my game plan and do something about it. I began to focus on laying out my plan and studying the system.

Game plan:

I asked questions and learned as much as I could about the draft process. I wanted to go into the air force as a lieutenant, so securing an officer's commission became my primary focus. I determined that the draft board promulgated a draft selection policy. So the draft board had jurisdiction over me until I got my degree.

I applied for an air force commission in a timely manner. To trump the draft board, I needed to hold my doctorate and officer's commission simultaneously. The trouble was that it took a while for my commission to come through and time was running out, as I was about to graduate from the university.

To get time on my side, I wrote formal questions to the draft board, inquiring about the policies related to my draft status. I did this because I knew the board met only once a month, which meant my letter of inquiry would bring me one month closer to graduation and my degree.

When the draft board responded, I would mail in other questions to give me another month. Their slow communications bought me extra time. I kept submitting questions until I held my degree and my officer's commission concurrently. With those two documents in hand, I thwarted the draft board's attempt to draft me as a private.

Dealing with the draft board highlighted the value of action over anger. I refused to spew out angry statements, and instead, kept a cool head and turned the system in my favor. I used questions to create *positive possibilities*. Listening and inquiry enabled me to face challenges in a result-oriented way.

What's important to understand about great accomplishments is that such things often take many little steps to get there, which requires patience to work through challenges along the way. I seldom embraced anger or other negative feelings but always looked for solutions. I always remembered to do things quietly, cerebrally, and without anger and frustration.

I think it's imperative not to give people any reason to define you in a negative way but as someone with a winning smile and a pleasant demeanor. People most often define you by how much you speak before thinking or by how you criticize others.

The person you're speaking to in casual conversation might one day be in a position to recommend you for a job or scholarship. Treat everyone you meet with respect, and you will be treated with respect in return.

In the face of adversity, ask advice of someone who has made it through a serious challenge. Those people can channel positive energies to guide you in the right direction.

During the bleakest days of the Civil Rights Movement, brave activists drew inspiration from the belief that they would "find a way out of no way."

That's the key—train your mind to look for *positive possibilities* in any situation, no matter how bleak it may seem. Tough situations test your character. Many people miss out on opportunities during tough times—discrimination, hard financial times, and countless other challenges. Just when it appears that all hope is lost, when the odds are against you, that's the time you need to shine.

Looking back, I view my challenges with the draft board as fortuitous. Just as I was leaving the safe, nurturing haven of Tuskegee, the draft board threw a cold bucket of water on my plans, reminding me that in the prejudiced world I was entering, I needed to work harder than my competitors to succeed. I had to be more patient and strategic than others.

I learned that power is not voluntarily given—personal freedom must be taken, sacrificed for, claimed, and defended. Power must be claimed with a cool, patient, and perceptive mind. My father did this during his quasi-enslavement on the racist plantation. He did the same when he stood down the KKK. My mother faced adversity with the same cool and calm attentiveness, the same bold grace.

From the earliest age, I was taught the value of diligently seeking a positive outcome from every situation. Had my parents and circumstances not instilled those survival skills in me, I might have been drafted into the military as a private, which would have been a major setback. I factored all I had learned into every aspect of my life. Now everything I think about by day and dream about at night, I put into my master planning process.

Tuskegee gave me invaluable professionalization and training, even more than a rich education. I met my lifelong mentor, Dr. Frederick K. Patterson, and my lifelong love and partner, Roberta Jones-Jenkins.

With the map for my future printed in my mind and heart, Tuskegee was the place I always reflected upon. It was a place of vision, a literal and symbolic home to any person who would accept its value system. It nurtured any student, especially any black student, who dared to dream. It helped me bear the weight of sacrifice and turn it into the joy of solid success.

CHAPTER 14

·❧·

Above the Fray: From the Arctic Circle to the Golden State

After outwitting the draft board, I graduated from Tuskegee in May 1957. Armed with my doctorate of veterinary medicine degree, I accepted a job with the US Agricultural Research Service in Massachusetts. My job was to travel the state testing cattle for various contagious bovine diseases. The job made it possible to support myself and bank a little money in the months before deploying to the air force. I enjoyed working that job and had set a record for conducting the most tests in a single day. When you love what you do, it's easy to do it well.

·❧·

I finally got my commission and reported for air force officers' training at Maxwell-Gunter Air Force Base in Montgomery, Alabama. I was one step closer to moving to California with my new bride.

When I finished the six weeks of training, I filled out an application that asked me where I wanted to be sent for assignment. I listed every base in California. Just the thought of Roberta and me together in California filled me with excitement.

While growing up, I constantly read about the extraordinary beauty and opportunity of the golden state, and one way or the other,

I was making my way to California. When I raised the issue with my Pentagon official, he made me a deal.

"If you go up to Greenland and do all right for the first year of duty, then in your second year, you can hang your shingle in California or wherever you want."

With mixed emotions, I watched the Greenland presentation with the other officers. The photo presentation showed a series of frozen images from Thule Air Base, which was seven hundred miles to the north and surrounded by ice and emptiness. Located halfway between Moscow and New York, that iced-covered country, alone between the Arctic and Atlantic oceans, made Thule a formidable and forbidding place. The glacier-topped world seen from above was a haze of wind-blown glacial silt. There was nothing but the base, the bay, and what appeared to be thousands of miles of rock and ice.

The slide show was paused at one point, and we were warned that the sun sets last in late October and wouldn't rise again until the end of February. I shivered but straightened up right quick. I would soon enough face the howling subzero winds at Thule, for I was surely on my way to one of the coldest and most undesirable tours of duty in the air force. But my future depended on it, so I took a deep, warm breath and steeled myself for the challenge ahead. *Greenland, here I come!*

What I didn't know then was that the military routinely sent minority veterinarians to the most isolated places in the world. One of my schoolmates was sent to Alaska, and another was assigned to the Middle East. Even after finding out that a disproportionate number of black officers were assigned to those locations, I agreed to go to Greenland. I had been offered a deal, and I was going to keep my end of the bargain, especially since it ended in California with my beautiful wife.

I took my brother Levaughn for company on the long drive to McGuire Air Force Base in New Jersey, and from there flew to Greenland, a cold and unforgiving place at the top of the world, next door to Russia. I arrived at two o'clock in the morning, which looked like high noon in the states because of Greenland's midnight sun. Unlike beautiful sunny California, four months of total light followed by four months of total darkness was going to take some getting used to.

The buildings were like deep freezers, built on permafrost, and because the winds blew 70 to 150 miles an hour, they were connected by thick ropes to assure safe passage between them. When the temperature fell from twenty to thirty degrees below freezing, we wore heavy boots called mukluks, iron pants, heavy lined overalls, and parkas that kept us relatively warm, the key term being *relative*.

Due to the isolation, many air force personnel couldn't handle the stress. People were constantly being shipped back to the States for psychiatric care. We lived in the hospital and bought ten-cent drinks in the officers' bar. Several of our men became alcoholics.

One of the things that kept people sane was mail. Mail kept us connected to home, and home was what we all yearned for. Roberta and I wrote each other every day. By that time, she had graduated from college and was studying for a graduate degree in nutrition at Beth Israel Hospital in Boston. Her letters not only kept me sane and connected, but also they increased my love and desire for my wife. We couldn't wait to be together again.

To kill time on weekends, we played cards, mostly dirty hearts. My foursome consisted of George, a good career man from Merced, California; Jim, a big red southerner from Louisiana; John, a dentist we referred to as Dollar; and myself.

Dollar was a mama's boy who had a hard time adjusting. There were times I had to run him out of my room because I got so tired of listening to his complaints. Sending him to his quarters didn't bother him one bit, because early the next morning, he would be right back in my space. I never did know why that Polish dentist from Chicago wanted to spend so much time with me. I guess it really didn't matter because soon enough we'd both leave for our individual assignments.

My main duties were to inspect the food supply coming from Dover Air Base in Delaware. I also cared for the sentry dogs, mostly large German shepherds. We had underground missiles in silos that could be activated to intercept any Russian aggression, and the dogs and their handlers secured the missile sites. My job was to keep those animals healthy, so I examined and treated them daily.

In addition to the military dogs, there were native Greenlanders' dogs that needed care. There were also foxes in the vicinity. In reviewing base records, I noticed that dogs and foxes had been dying from an unknown disease in the area. I sent tissue samples to labs in the states for examination, but all the reports came back negative. I sent more samples with the same results. The news was very disappointing. Something had to be wrong, and I could not figure out what it was.

I wrote to Roberta, which always lifted my spirits.

"Hello good looking,

If we stay the course this year, I'll be free to choose a station in California for my next year. That's where we will grow our love, our business, and our children in the sunshine. I've been reading about that place since high school, and I know you're going to like it.

I think sunshine will be good for lovers like us. What say you?

Write tomorrow.

MJ"

CHAPTER 15

⋯⋯

Rabies under the Midnight Sun

I was told that Greenland was the coldest and most undesirable duty in the military, and after living for a year in that country on the Arctic Circle, with its monolithic ice sheet covering all its landmass except the coastlands, I had to agree.

I could have gotten bitter about my assignment, but I knew better. I had trained my mind to persevere and never let myself forget that a job well done in Greenland meant my next stop would be California.

In response to the escalating Cold War, the US military constructed Thule Air Base in Greenland to house and protect silos containing nuclear missiles aimed at the Soviet Union. The guard dogs were part of the first line of defense should war break out. With their thick winter coats and superior senses, the German shepherds were trusted allies for the human guards, and I remained diligent in monitoring and maintaining the dogs' health and strength.

Every time, I would pull on my parka, mukluks, iron pants, and venture out into the arctic elements. Putting on all that gear was a real process, but it kept me warm in winds that blew ice, sleet, and snow while I rambled around in a jeep, carrying out my on-and-off-base duties.

The hospital and other buildings were built on stilts, which enabled the powerful winds to blow around all sides of each structure.

I spent the majority of my days and nights in the hospital building, which housed not only the animal clinic, but also my bedroom, a cafeteria, and a bar. Many days and nights could pass before I would ever step outside, but focus on my duties kept me sane during those months of constant darkness.

The alarming number of foxes and dogs that kept dying for some unknown reason occupied all my attention. I asked for permission to start an experimental program to study and determine the mysterious cause of the animal deaths. The CO granted me authority to assemble a team of six hospital aides to investigate the problem.

We went out to observe the guard dogs and wild foxes, looking for signs of illness. I had a hunch that the animals were dying of rabies. In veterinary school, I had studied rabies in depth but had never seen an actual case, as rabies had been virtually eradicated in the United States.

Soon, we observed that some dogs and foxes looked as if they might have early onset of rabies—mouths slack and open, eyes glazed over, and aimless, unwary behavior. So my team and I captured them and brought them back to the clinic to observe for twenty-four hours around the clock. I directed each shift of aides to record animal observations every ten minutes.

The animals all died.

◄◄❈►►

After analyzing all the symptoms, I became more certain than ever that the dogs and foxes had rabies. I called headquarters in Westover Air Force Base, Massachusetts, and presented my hypothesis. The people in charge at headquarters said that it was too cold for the rabies virus to grow in Greenland. Still, I was certain it was rabies. All the symptoms were there.

When I had received my doctorate at the Tuskegee Institute, I had taken the following oath: *Being admitted to the profession of veterinary medicine, I solemnly dedicate myself and the knowledge I possess to the benefit of society, to the conservation of our livestock resources, and to the relief of suffering of animals. I will practice my profession consciously with dignity. The health of my patients, the best interest of their owners, and the welfare of my fellow man will be my primary consideration. I will, at all times, be humane and temper pain with anesthesia where indicated. I will not use my knowledge contrary to the laws of humanity, nor in contravention to the ethical code of my profession. I will uphold and strive to advance the honor and noble traditions of the veterinary profession. These pledges I make freely in the eyes of God and upon my honor.*

I took that oath seriously and felt it was my ethical duty to get to the bottom of what was killing so many animals in Greenland. To test my hypothesis, I sent several fox and dog heads to headquarters in Massachusetts to test for any Negri bodies in the hippocampus region of the animal brains, which would confirm rabies. Rabies is usually confirmed by running lab tests on the head of the dead animal in question.

The tests came back negative, but I remained convinced that rabies was the reason for the animals' deaths. It didn't make sense to me why the tests were turning up negative. I wrote to headquarters and asked if I could send my samples to the World Health Organization laboratory in London. To my surprise, the top officer at headquarters gave me the okay.

The first head I sent to London came back positive for rabies. When that report came back, sirens went off. This discovery went against the long-standing military position that Greenland was simply too cold for rabies to exist. The office of the US Secretary of Defense wrote to me and stated that under no circumstances, due to national security, could I discuss anything regarding rabies or any other disease in Greenland.

I complied with this secret protocol but immediately began developing my game plan to eradicate rabies in Greenland. The air force granted me access to two helicopter crews to conduct the research throughout Greenland. I was the first person to discover rabies in that country, a discovery all the more important when we learned rabies was also killing people.

To address the outbreak, I initiated a Rabies Eradication Program and flew all over the country vaccinating animals and assessing the severity of the rabies outbreak. After implementing the eradication program for the entire country, I formally wrote my findings and sent it through the appropriate military channels for publication.

A few weeks later, I received a rewritten version of my report, littered with inaccuracies. Most alarming was my discovery that two high-ranking officials had taken credit for the report. Their names were written on the top of the report, and my name, written in smaller print, had been moved to the very end.

I went to talk with my commanding officer. "Look at this," I said, handing him the original report and the rewritten version. "They intend to take credit for these findings."

He was struck silent for a moment and then said, "Well, let's call those SOBs up and curse them out."

I laughed. "I'm a captain, sir. Cussing them out is above my pay grade."

Meanwhile, I kicked in a major game plan—stay cool, refrain from anger or panic, and figure out how to get credit for the research I had done. I was the first person to discover rabies in Greenland and the founder of the Rabies Eradication Program. I knew publishing those findings would be a tremendous boost for my career, and I was going to get what I deserved! Nothing less, nothing more.

In the days and weeks that followed, I asked questions and carefully assessed my options. I used the same tactics I implemented to prevent the draft board from inducting me into the air force as a private before I got my doctorate of veterinary medicine degree.

My game plan was in motion: I started writing to my superiors who sought to take credit for my work and asked them questions about the article. It took about two weeks' turnaround for them to answer each inquiry. Every time I got a response, I'd raise questions about another part of the report. Since I had done all the work and they didn't know anything about my research, I had the upper hand.

In dealing with the draft board and later with those high-ranking military officers, I used questions to claim my liberty and reach my career goals. I had learned that in many cases, what seemed like an immediate problem could be delayed by legitimate and legal channels of inquiry. I learned that delay could offer an incredible strategy for using time to overcome the problem. My game plan was working.

CHAPTER 16

The Royal Promise Turns Sour

After serving a year in Greenland, my new post in California was within reach, and I was excited. I had followed through on my end of the bargain by serving Greenland with distinction. But the military threw me a curveball. Rather than send me to California as promised, the air force commissioned me to Oscoda, Michigan, at Wurtsmith Air Force Base, a station in northern Michigan near Lake Huron. If there was any place colder than Greenland, it had to be Oscoda.

I was fighting mad, but my game plan kept me from becoming angry and spewing out my inner feelings. It helped that Roberta would join me in Michigan, so together, we would make the best of it. The air force had reneged on its promise, and there was nothing we could do to change that. But the game plan was to control our attitudes, and we did.

My duties in Michigan were similar to those in Greenland: overseeing food inspection and tending to a sentry of German shepherds that guarded military fighter jets.

During what would be my final year in the air force, I searched for ways to publish my research related to discovering rabies in Greenland and establishing the Rabies Eradication Program. I laid out my plan, but there were other factors even more important to me. The Vietnam War was raging, and I felt so strongly about it that I resigned my commission.

But that doesn't mean I was going to give up.

The very day I got out of the military, I wrote my own article, put my name at the top, and left the other officials out. I submitted it to the official journals of the American Veterinary Medical Association and the World Health Organization, and my article appeared in the August 1960 issue of the *Journal of the American Veterinary Medical Association*. Soon after, the World Health Organization published my findings, which gave my research international exposure.

Reprint from the JOURNAL of the American Veterinary Medical Association, Vol. 137, No. 3, August 1, 1960, pp. 183-185.

Rabies Discovered in Greenland

Matthew JENKINS, D.V.M.
Kjeld WAMBERG, D.V.M.

THIS REPORT describes the first confirmed laboratory diagnosis of rabies in animals in Greenland. Rabies in man has not been reported in that country but, due to the close association of dogs and man, it may have occurred.

It has been argued that rabies is unlikely to occur in man in cold climates because the heavy clothing worn most of the time would prohibit saliva from entering wounds inflicted by rabid animals. The validity of this argument has not been determined.

History

During the fall of 1958, we examined 11 dogs, 6 of which had been bitten by other dogs and 5 by foxes. No signs of rabies appeared in any of the 11 dogs during the 14 days they were quarantined.

Greenland is heavily populated with foxes which have moved near military bases in search of food. When the potential health hazard of foxes was realized, the Greenland Health Department made available all of its information on diseases transmissible from animals to man, including incidence of rabies in arctic climates, clinical signs, course, predisposition, prevention, and treatment.

This information included reports on a disease characterized by fits (and called "fits") which had been recognized for the past 100 years. Since 1906, periodic studies

Dr. Jenkins, Animal Industry Division, Bureau of Poultry Inspection for California, Monterey Park. Dr. Wamberg is associate professor, Royal Veterinary and Agriculture College, Copenhagen, Denmark, and veterinary adviser in the Greenland Department, Copenhagen, Denmark.

The information in this article was obtained during 1958 and 1959 while Dr. Jenkins was stationed at Thule Air Base, Greenland.

The authors acknowledge the cooperation of the Greenland Government, through the efforts of Dr. J. Giståud. Further acknowledgement is made of the laboratory assistance provided by the Virus and Rickettsia Laboratory, U. S. Public Health Service, Montgomery, Ala.

The contents of this article reflect the authors' personal views and are not to be construed as a statement of Air Force policy.

had been made of this condition, but no diagnosis of rabies was ever confirmed.

Although goverment officials of Greenland stated that rabies was not known to occur in that country, they recommended treating animal bites as though rabies were involved. All base personnel were warned that foxes might be rabid.

On Nov. 24, 1958, a fox which attacked a team of sled dogs was killed and the brain examined for rabies lesions. No Negri bodies were found. A brain suspension was injected into 3 mice, 1 of which died 12 days following injection; the other 2 died 18 days later. No Negri bodies were found in the 3 mice. Shortly after this negative report was received, the 5 dogs which had been attacked by the fox showed signs of rabies and died within a short time. It was impossible to retrieve the heads of the dogs, because the Greenlanders had burned the bodies.

On Dec. 22, 1958, another dog was bitten by a fox and the fox's head was submitted for laboratory examination. No Negri bodies were found in the brain, nor in the brains of mice which were subsequently inoculated with a suspension of the fox's brain.

In February, 1959, we were informed by the Danish health inspector that fits in foxes and dogs had reached epizootic proportions in some areas and threatened the existence of the native Greenlanders. In northern Greenland, the people are dependent on the services of their sled dogs to secure food, and they are with their dogs most of the time. Although fits had existed in their dogs for many years, the Greenlanders seemed to have adjusted to this problem by immediately killing and burning any dog at the first signs of this condition.

During the latter part of February, 1959, a research project was initiated to ascertain the cause of fits, which clinically resembled rabies.

Methods and Results

Specimens 852, 853, and 854. On May 16, 1959, 3 heads of animals which had had fits were submitted for laboratory examination. These heads were marked 852-black dog, 853-brown dog, and 854-silver fox. The excised brains were placed in separate Petri dishes and stored at 4 C. The following day, suspensions were made from

Securing publication of my research gave me national and international credibility, a very big boost for my early career. My research in Greenland and subsequent publication of that work caused Tuskegee University to give me an honorary doctorate in Science in 2011.

The military, however, never gave me any recognition for my discovery of rabies in Greenland. At that point, though, my former superiors who tried to claim my research as their own couldn't touch me. They were only a bad memory from my past.

I never heard from the air force again, but that experience reinforced my belief that a less powerful person picking a fight in the face of injustice is usually hopeless. It's better to stay cool, ask questions, and find a way to win. I chose that route rather than fight with my superiors, with all those stars and medals on their shoulders. I chose to outsmart them by concentrating on *positive possibilities* to overcome an abusive situation.

And the fact remained that if I had displayed a bitter attitude toward Greenland in reaction to the air force sending me there in the first place, I would have missed out on one of the most important discoveries in my entire veterinary career—the discovery of rabies in Greenland!

Fifty years after completing my year of military service at Thule Air Base, I returned to Greenland. Roberta and I went on a nine-country cruise, and the ship stopped over. After a half century of seeing that rugged land of colossal glaciers, fierce winds, and twenty-four-hour days of unrelenting light and dark, it felt surreal to be back.

Memories rushed in as we landed, and I eyed a little gas station on a short stretch away from our debarkation point. I walked over and asked the attendant if he knew if rabies was still active on the island. His eyes lit up, and he told me that I should speak with a veterinarian who lived around the corner! I was curious to hear what he had to say.

I followed the attendant's directions and was soon knocking on the front door of a Greenland residence. A woman answered the door. I introduced myself and told her that I'd heard a veterinarian who had dealt with rabies eradication on the island lived there. Her eyes lit up just as the gas station attendants had, so I was doubly curious.

"My husband would love to speak with you," she said. "I will call him right now."

Moments later, she handed me her telephone receiver. The man on the other end of the line said, "Dr. Jenkins, you're my hero!"

It turned out that the man on the phone was the veterinarian who had replaced me after I left Thule Air Base more than fifty years ago! He had come to Greenland to serve at Thule and extended his stay for another year and ended up marrying a local woman, the woman who'd answered the door. After completing his military duties, he was hired by the Danish Government, the overseers of the Greenland Government.

Long ago, I had given up on receiving any positive acknowledgement from the US Air Force for my work in Greenland, which made this unexpected conversation all the more gratifying. He told me that he had read all my articles and used many of the protocols for eradicating rabies that I had developed years ago.

That was a moment of sheer elation!

It's amazing how hard work and dedication can pay off long after the work has been done and in the most unexpected ways.

Matthew Jenkins Photo Journey through the Years

The Jenkins family home in Loxley, Alabama

Azalee Jenkins Henderson, sister

Consuello Jenkins Harper, sister

Johnetta Jenkins, sister

Left to right Brothers Matthew, Levaughn,
Joyful, Samuel, Shelley and Hilliard

Oldest brother John Wesley Jenkins, Jr.

Siblings Samuel, Johnetta, Matthew,
Consuello (Connie), Levaughn

The Jenkins Family at daughter Sabrae's
graduation from Howard University.
(from left to right: Dexter, Matthew, Sabrae, Derryl and Roberta)

Our youngest son Dexter, his wife Della, son Dominic,
Roberta, Matthew and daughter Bianca

Bianca and Dominic Jenkins (Dexter's daughter and son)

Olivia Jenkins (Derryl's daughter), Bianca and
Dominic Jenkins (Dexter's daughter and son)

From left to right - Derryl with daughter Olivia and son Zowey

Olivia Jenkins – daughter of Derryl Jenkins

Zowey Jenkins – son of Derryl Jenkins

Daughter Sabrae Derby and her family: Husband
Brian, sons Amaris and Makarios, Sabrae

Makarios and Amaris Derby

Roberta, Richard and Yvonne Fink and
Matthew at their chalet in Austria

Matt and Roberta skiing in Austria with the Finks

Dr. Matthew Jenkins with US Senator Bob Graham of Texas

Dr. Matthew Jenkins with President Ronald Reagan

Dr. and Mrs. Matthew Jenkins with
Secretary of State Hillary Clinton

Dr. Matthew Jenkins with President Barack Obama

Founding Board Members of the Educational
Foundation for African Americans (now called The
Matthew and Roberta Jenkins Family Foundation)
Front row from left to right: Roberta Jenkins,
Elaine Redfield, Dr. Frederick Patterson
Back row: Sabrae Derby, Douglas Freeman, Matthew Jenkins, Los
Angeles Mayor Tom Bradley, Reynold Neufeld and James Rigby

From:
Claremont
Graduate
University
Magazine
2002

Dr. Matthew Jenkins
President
S.D.D. Enterprises, Inc.
President, Educational
Foundation for African
Americans
CGU Board of Trustees
and

Roberta Jenkins
Vice President
S.D.D. Enterprises, Inc.
Vice President
Educational Foundation for
African Americans
Board of Visitors
School of Educational Studies

Matt and Roberta Jenkins have supported CGU for almost two decades. They have contributed greatly through their financial support and their involvement as Board members at CGU. Matt Jenkins began his career as a veterinarian, moved into real estate development, and is now serving on numerous non-profit boards. Roberta Jenkins co-founded S.D.D. Enterprises and the Educational Foundation for African Americans with Matt. She was a founding board member of the Orange County Music Center and is also active in many community organizations. The Jenkins have devoted themselves to improving educational opportunities for African American students at CGU, California State University Fullerton and through the Drew Saturday Science Academy.

10 HABIT OF THE HEART

115

GARY AMBROSE

Matt and Roberta Jenkins talk about Educational Foundation for Black Americans.

Fullerton Couple Realize Their Dream of Extending Aid to Black Students

By DOUG BROWN, *Times Staff Writer*

When Matt Jenkins was working his way through college during the '50s, he had to get up at 3 a.m. to clean animal laboratories. Today Jenkins, 52, a millionaire real estate developer, still rises at about the same time.

He then sets out from his hillside home overlooking Fullerton for a pre-dawn jog with his wife and business partner, Roberta, 48. Their conversation often turns to how their good fortune stems largely from **ORANGE COUNTY** the scholarships, loans and jobs that paid Matt's way through Tuskegee University, a 3,400-student, predominantly black college founded a century ago in Alabama.

The Jenkinses, both of whom are Tuskegee University graduates, last year established the Educational Foundation for Black Americans in an attempt to give the current generation of black youth the opportunity to go to college. They have donated $150,000 to help the new organization get off the ground.

There are other groups, most notably the United Negro College Fund, that raise money for higher education for blacks. However, the Jenkinses, during a recent interview in the family room of their Sunny Hills home, explained that they set up their foundation a year ago with their own vision of how college educations for blacks should be funded.

They believed it was time for those blacks who had benefited most from university educations—successful black professionals and entrepreneurs like themselves—to assume the financial and moral responsibility for educating and motivating today's generation of young blacks.

Affluent blacks would take this leadership role, the Jenkinses believed, by tapping financial resources available through their network of contacts in the professional and business worlds, both in the black and white communities.

The Jenkinses said they feared that if black professionals failed to take on this responsibility, no one else would.

"Today there are fewer blacks in the nation attending college than [there were] 10 years ago because of cutbacks in federal funding of higher education," Matt said.

"One can only wonder what's going to happen to young people who're being denied even the opportunity of a college education, though they're

Please see ASSISTANCE, Page 24

Los Angeles Times

VIEW

Orange County

• Sunday, December 15, 1985 / Part VI

116

Matthew Jenkins Receives Honorary Degree

Hundreds of Tuskegee University alumni and other school supporters gathered at the University Chapel for the Charter Day/Homecoming Convocation on Sunday, November 6, during Homecoming Weekend activities. Alumnus Archon Matthew Jenkins of Orange County, California's Epsilon Epsilon Boulé was the keynote speaker. After his address, he was presented with an honorary doctor-of-science degree by university president Gilbert L. Rochon. A former member of Tuskegee's board of trustees, Archon Jenkins received a doctorate in veterinary medicine from Tuskegee in 1957. He retired from veterinary medicine in 1979 to devote himself full-time to SDD Enterprises as its president and CEO. He is currently the firm's chairman.

Acknowledging that "my DNA is deeply embedded in Mother Tuskegee," Archon Jenkins recounted how he was reluctant to leave his duties at his family's farm and follow his mother's wish for him to attend the university: "I was literally devastated because I was having so much fun. I realize many years later she had much more wisdom than me."

He described the lessons he learned from his mother as the foundation for his family's philanthropy. "Always give service to humanity. That's who we are," Archon Jenkins said. "That's how we were taught. We don't know any better." He and his Archousa, Roberta, founded the Matthew and Roberta Jenkins Family Foundation in 1984 to provide financial assistance to African American institutions. To date, the foundation has distributed more than $10 million. Archon Jenkins and Archousa Roberta have also given to Tuskegee and sponsored the recent campus hotel renovations.

In his address, Archon Jenkins encouraged others to make monetary, legacy or service gifts to Tuskegee. He said that the university's capital campaign needs support and cited other areas where it would be especially helpful, including organization and communication and public

Archon Matthew Jenkins (center) receives an honorary degree.

relations. "If we're going to meet this challenge, we all have to pitch in," he said.

Archon Jenkins argued that a campus-wide change in attitude is key to Tuskegee's success. He urged all faculty and staff to be personable ambassadors of the university and to do their jobs with professionalism and passion. In addition, he stressed that employees should want to show the best that they can offer. "We want that 'wow' factor not just from President Rochon but from everyone," he said.

Archon Gerald I. West
Grapter, Epsilon Epsilon Boulé

Dr. Matthew Jenkins on stage in the play Showboat

Being honored at UNCF's Inaugural Mayors Masked Ball
Los Angeles Mayor Antonio Villaraigosa, Matthew
Jenkins, Roberta Jenkins and Dr. Michael
Lomax President and CEO of UNCF

Dr. Matthew Jenkins speaking at the Century Plaza Hotel
in Los Angeles after being honored by Compton College

Dr. and Mrs. Matthew Jenkins being
honored at Compton College

At the dedication of my new hospital opening
(from left to right: Compton Mayor, Chester Crain,
Dr. Matthew Jenkins, and friend Pliny Jenkins)

At my home in Fullerton, CA. In front my wife Roberta.
From left to right Jan Bergquist, Craig Bergquist, Richard
Fink and Carl Bergquist. All are skiing partners.

At the beginning of the civil rights movement: North Carolina A&T College students sit-in at F.W. Woolworth lunch counter, Greensboro, North Carolina 1960

Race Relations Conference, Highlander Folk School, Monteagle, Tennessee (late 1950s) Dr. Frederick Patterson (center in white shirt) with Rosa Parks (to the left), who triggered the Montgomery, Alabama bus boycott led by Dr. Martin Luther King, Jr. Roberta and I participated in civil rights demonstrations with Dr. King.

CHAPTER 17

◦⟨⟩◦

My Mega Game Plan:
Seven Days a Week, Seven Years—
Morning, Noon, and Night

At last!

Roberta and I finished our individual training, and I was free from military commitments. After serving active duty, it was normal protocol to transfer into reserve status. But I was so adamantly opposed to the Vietnam War that I had resigned my commission. This was done quietly, because to advertise my sentiments about the war could have branded me as a communist. About the same time, Muhammad Ali, Dr. Martin Luther King, Jr., and other prominent Americans had revealed their disdain for the war effort and been branded as such.

My service officially ended in April 1960.

Roberta and I packed our belongings and drove west, heading for northern California with our white poodle, Gigi. We drove directly to Sacramento, looking for employment in the state's capital city. The clerk looked at me over his bifocals, the freckles on his nose standing out against his skin. "There's only one open position in the whole state that requires veterinary skills," he said.

"I'm listening," I answered.

"It's a temporary position inspecting chicken slaughterhouses near Los Angeles."

It wasn't ideal, but I was in no position to be picky. The biggest problem was the southern California part. I had planned to live in northern California. I met with the chief veterinarian and told him I would return the next day and let him know if I wanted the position.

That night, Roberta and I discussed our options and agreed that it made sense to take the position in southern California. It would be foolish to follow a game plan that had no job prospects in northern California. The next morning, I returned to the State House and accepted the position. And off we drove to southern California.

It was time to set my game plan for the next phase of my career. There were many uncertainties, but my number one priority was to own a veterinary practice in California. That clarity brought me to an essential declaration: *if you know what you want to do, do it!*

I knew the longer I spent inspecting slaughterhouses, the better I would become at doing that. But I also felt that each day I didn't have my own practice was another day without progress. After I had worked for the state of California for four months, my supervisor called me in to his office.

"Jenkins, you're doing an excellent job here. You make it easy for all of us. So if you stay on for two more months, you'll become permanent."

It made sense to keep the job. Even so, I remembered something my brother Samuel told me about my father's remarks to a fellow employee who cautioned him against quitting his supervisor's job on the railroad. "If I'm worth a dollar a day to the railroad, I'm worth a whole lot more to myself." I felt the same way. I wanted my own practice. I knew I could always go back to the slaughterhouse job if I had to.

I decided this was a good time to start looking for a place to practice and find part-time work with a veterinarian. I wasn't particular about what kind of work I would be doing.

After being out of school for three years, I needed to take the California state board exams so I could practice veterinary medicine in California. To make sure I passed the exams, I got up at three o'clock every morning before work to re-read all my veterinary books. I studied until I could recall all the topics I had in veterinary school. I knew that hard work was an essential ingredient for succeeding in this endeavor.

Every challenge is an opportunity for me to become more disciplined, more focused, and more productive. I passed my boards.

Then I started my search for part-time work while looking for a place to open my own practice. The first day I went out searching for extra work at veterinary offices, I found one doctor who was in his office just before lunch hour. When I told his receptionist that I was a veterinarian myself and wanted to see the doctor, she took me right in to meet him. The doctor and I exchanged professional talk about the practice of veterinary medicine in Los Angeles County. It seemed like an easy exchange. Then I asked if he knew of any vet who wanted to rent me his office.

"No, I don't," he said.

"Do you know any veterinarian who might need to hire a part-time vet?" I asked.

The doctor hesitated, and his demeanor changed. He shifted in his seat and finally stood.

"There are several doctors around here who might be able to use you occasionally. But you'd have to work in the back so the pet owners wouldn't know you."

"So the color of my skin would matter to the owners of these animals?"

He nodded sheepishly.

I turned around and walked out without another word, more determined than ever to start my own practice. I later found out that some of my classmates had encountered the same experience.

Meanwhile, I kept up daily conversations with some of the salesmen in the area who visited animal clinics peddling supplies and medicine. I asked them to keep me informed of any veterinary practice that might come available for lease. I felt comfortable asking about a practice to lease because I literally ran the hospital during my internship in New York.

One day, I received a call from one of the drug salesmen about a veterinarian who would be teaching at a veterinary school in India. The doctor wanted to lease his practice for three years. I met with him, and we agreed on terms.

The first year, I doubled the income. I wrote the owner and asked if he would sell his practice to me, but he declined.

I began to look for land to build a veterinary hospital, and in three years, when the doctor returned to the states, I had built a new state-of-the-art veterinary hospital.

Before the clinic owner returned, I worked with a builder I found through the Tuskegee Institute Alumni Association. We spent considerable time in 1963 planning and designing the hospital. I thought about the comfort of my clients and focused on workplace efficiency. We piped in music and added intercom and air-conditioning throughout the building. It was a beautiful place, and I was looking forward to the future.

To my surprise, the veterinarian I'd leased from sued me for practicing too close to him. When I had purchased the lot, I thought it was far enough away, but obviously, he didn't feel the same.

Rather than become embroiled in a court battle, I empathized with the other veterinarian, and we settled the dispute out of court. I have learned that disputes are inevitable in business because not every person perceives things the same way. The key to settling such disputes is to find agreeable terms rather than fight about who is right or wrong. I viewed the settlement that I paid the veterinarian as the cost of doing business. That approach restored goodwill between us, and we got along fine after that.

When I started my own veterinary practice, I noticed that most of the doctors would work only from 9:00 a.m. to 6:00 p.m. and didn't want to take night calls. There were no emergency animal clinics around, so I saw a huge opportunity, a real *positive possibility* to grow my practice. I called local veterinarians and asked them to refer any night or weekend calls to me.

For the first seven years of my practice, I worked normal office hours and took night and weekend calls seven days a week. That was my 7–7 plan: seven days a week for seven years.

One thing I addressed in speeches to business and community groups was the importance of finding the competitive edge in any situation. Education and practical knowledge paired with a tenacious work ethic is a great formula for success. But implementing that winning formula requires sacrifice. My seven days a week and night calls for seven years served as the game plan. I set up and wrote my plan and then applied the steps every day for seven years. I never slacked off. Few others would take up that assignment, no matter how lucrative the possibilities.

My wife was an equal partner in our struggles and successes. The day when I went into the office, I told her, "I want to work this practice for twenty years, and then I want to be out."

Roberta understood that my goals extended beyond a lifetime of working. She also knew that my veterinary practice was designed to become the engine that would propel us to larger entrepreneurial goals—to retire from my veterinary practice at the age of forty-five, to pursue an investment in real estate and other entrepreneurial ventures, to raise a great family, to travel the world, and to form a philanthropic foundation to acknowledge and honor Dr. Fredrick Patterson who had advised me so well during my college years.

I meditated on those goals and my game plan as I moved forward. It was burned into my consciousness. The 7–7 plan gave me the best odds of generating the most powerful economic engine to power my future enterprises.

Implementing my 7–7 plan would have been impossible without Roberta's support. Many times, she and I would get dressed up for a night out, and I'd get a call that a client had been referred to my emergency service. I would invariably go to the hospital and perform the surgery. She never complained. In fact, many times, Roberta would come with me and help with the surgery. Her support meant everything.

One of my friends, a doctor, complained, "Every time I go to work after hours, my wife gives me hell."

Comments like that from my colleagues proved to me what I believed—that choosing the right mate determines your future together more than anything else. If you choose the wrong mate, you'll get pulled away from your goals and perhaps grow apart when you should be pulling together.

It turned out that when there were after-work emergencies or when working professionals were too busy to bring their pets into the office during office hours, my services were a great accommodation. Many of those pet owners didn't have a regular vet, but I was there, happy to serve them.

Soon, it was clear that I had tapped into a sweet spot in the local marketplace. The strong demand for after-hour and weekend veterinary service made for a perfect combination. That's when I began to place advertisements in the Long Beach Yellow Pages promoting my twenty-four-hour emergency service.

Starting with a small support staff, I conducted all the surgical procedures. One young woman named Carma Barret started working with me in those early years and stayed until I sold my practice in 1979. Carma didn't have a college degree, but she was very bright and responsible. She handled administrative duties and assisted me while I conducted surgical procedures. We were a heck of a team. I look back and marvel at how much work we could plow through. Over time, I hired other veterinarians and support staff and promoted Carma to office manager.

Hard work deserves to be rewarded.

My practice kept growing as I stuck to my 7–7 plan. Roberta's support remained steadfast. Over the years, my practice grew to a point where I had four doctors and a staff of eighteen people. Eventually, I purchased the lot next door to expand the hospital. That lot also had a house on it, which we leased to tenants.

While running my practice, I remained focused on pursuing my investment goals. I took night classes at Compton College to refine my understanding of the financial and legal fundamentals of buying and selling the right properties. And while I was eager to delve more into real estate, I also understood that my top priority was to maximize the profitability and efficiency of my veterinary practice.

I knew if I did that, it would set the stage for our future.

CHAPTER 18

❖

The X Factor: Emergency Clinics, Insurance, and an Anesthetic Breakthrough

As my practice grew, I actively sought new business possibilities. Based upon the strong demand for after-hour and weekend emergency services my practice offered, I knew there must be great demand for similar services in nearby communities. I studied the Los Angeles County map and considered how to attract clients from all cities surrounding my hospital in Compton.

I looked for a strong concentration of clients seeking an after-hour's service. By the address and zip code they filled out in their paperwork, I determined that an emergency clinic in North Long Beach could prove to be lucrative.

There was a fifteen-to-twenty-minute limit on the time a client would be willing to drive for veterinary service. Establishing an emergency clinic in North Long Beach would give me entree to the entire community. That clinic would open a large swath of Long Beach and the surrounding cities to my business.

I drove the freeways and side streets looking for a spot for an emergency clinic and found a promising location on Cherry Avenue, near the 91 Freeway in North Long Beach. It seemed ideal, as close freeway access was essential.

Expanding my practice with the emergency clinic was a calculated risk, but it succeeded because I did my marketing research. I am always amazed by would-be entrepreneurs who take big financial risks without doing their homework. Such gambits are not calculated risks, they are reckless ideas. I've always calculated risks by weighing them against the consumer demand for the goods or service I offered.

I factored in all the financial considerations by conducting a careful cost-benefit analysis. An investment is worthwhile if the opportunity is so promising you can't afford *not* to take the risk. I couldn't afford not to take that risk with my emergency clinic—and it worked.

Years ago on the farm, my mom and dad noticed that people needed gasoline for their vehicles, so they started to sell gas. They filled needs that helped benefit their customers and the community. I have always taken the same approach in all my business ventures, using the old adage: "Find a need and fill it."

In the 1970s, a group of local veterinarians got together and established Veterinary Pet Insurance (VPI), which grew into the largest such insurance company of its kind in the country. I was one of the original investors. Later, Nationwide Insurance purchased a controlling interest in VPI. I represented the veterinarians and worked with a lawyer who represented non-veterinarian investors. Together, we negotiated the sale of the remaining shares to Nationwide Insurance.

Why did I take such a proactive role in launching pet insurance? I saw a need. Over the years, I observed many situations where clients lacked the funds to pay for surgical procedures for their pets. It was clear that not all clients were able to spend a lot of money on their animals. But if they had insurance, they could make a small payment each month and finance a necessary operation for their beloved pets. Now any client who wanted to pay for their pet's treatment could do so, and that arrangement would improve the profitability of my practice.

I called some of my veterinary colleagues to tell them why I was investing in pet insurance and how I thought they should consider doing the same. None of them was interested. So I moved on. It was their loss because the pet insurance program kept growing.

Later, I poured over research on pet insurance in other countries and found that a significant percentage of people in the United Kingdom paid for pet insurance. At that time, only three or four percent of people in the United States had pet insurance. That told me there was a strong potential for growth in domestic markets. I never hinder my potential by saying, "Well, it's never been done before."

Many doctors know a lot about their particular specializations, but take them outside of their technical field and they're like babes in the woods. I never let myopia set in or do I become complacent. I am always inquisitive, always learning about a broad range of subjects.

Proactive inquisitiveness is key to spotting entrepreneurial opportunities. I developed a new anesthetic combination simply by refining an existing practice. When I was doing surgeries on cats and dogs, I had one anesthesia that worked rapidly but lasted only a short time. I had another that lasted longer, but it took a long time to take effect. The problem with the long-term anesthesia was that it took animals a long time to regain consciousness and move around, which was the opposite of the desired recovery.

One day, it occurred to me, "Why not mix the anesthetics together?" I used that experiment on animals that were to be euthanized, and it worked like a charm. The combined anesthetics knocked animals down immediately, and the animals woke up after the surgeries much more quickly. That was huge because it's ideal for the animal to get up as soon as possible after surgery. I published my findings in *Modern Veterinary Practice Magazine* and received letters from veterinarians around the world thanking me for the innovation.

Being innovative is one of the great joys of any enterprise. I tell young people that they should never become satisfied with the status quo. Often, when people think about what career to pursue, they think about huge discoveries, like inventing some revolutionary technology. That's a possibility, but the vast majority of entrepreneurial opportunities lie within meeting practical needs in a more efficient manner.

Look at most computer innovations: they involve the gradual reduction of size while incrementally increasing speed and memory. Simply reducing the time it takes to conduct a technical or medical procedure by twenty or thirty percent can be a game changer. The idea is to identify a need and fill it. That's how I assessed the value of pet insurance. A lot of people didn't think much of it then, but now it's a big thing.

Ask yourself: what are the needs in my profession, my career, my home, and society in general? Bette Nesmith Graham was a typist who could have remained satisfied with her profession, which included retyping an entire page every time she made an error. But Graham decided to innovate and developed Liquid Paper. What started as an experiment in her kitchen turned into a business she sold later for nearly fifty million dollars.

All entrepreneurs are dreamers, but not all entrepreneurs succeed. Those who succeed know how to translate their dreams into goals with the corresponding game plan to reach them. That's why it is essential to read and learn from reputable sources about a wide range of topics that are grounded in reality. Grounding ensures that entrepreneurial inspiration is rooted in an understanding of its use and benefits. With a firm grasp on that reality, it is possible to set achievable goals rather than impossible dreams.

Many people set only lofty goals. They want to be a movie star, a famous musician, or a professional athlete. Such goals are possible but unlikely. As they say, "If it were easy, then everyone would do it."

For example, I could have been a very good football player. I played well in high school. I was good, but I didn't have time to play in college. So I set my game plan to make my first million dollars by grounding my goals in reality.

My research showed that most American millionaires, during that time span, gained their wealth in real-estate investments, not professional sports. I perceived that becoming a veterinarian would be difficult but doable if I applied myself. Establishing a successful veterinary practice would enable me to transition to my second career in real-estate investment.

If you remain deeply grounded in the world of probable ideas, you will pursue doable goals. In the end, doable goals are more exciting than improbable goals because they lead, more often than not, to positive results. And positive results are exciting. What's doubly exciting is that two or three interrelated goals can lead to *big results*. That's why I learned to keep my head out of the clouds, to make sure I wasn't just dreaming up impossibilities. My dreams are always achievable.

I always had a deep feeling of positivity and confidence; I believed I could improve any situation. I filled my thinking with self-assurance. If my wife tells me something is broken, I tell her, "I can fix it." I feel that way because most challenges boil down to common sense.

When I was a kid on the farm, I knew I could fix engines, plows, and other things because they had been repaired before. Know-how plus diligence is my winning formula. If I don't have the know-how, I find it with research. I read books, take classes, and learn from others who are experts in my subject of interest.

If a person feels he or she can do something, usually, they can. They might not always do it right the first time, but with perseverance, they'll find a way. The alternative is a nonstarter. If you say you can't, you won't. The horse never gets out of the gate, the ship never sets sail, and the universe of *positive possibilities* turns to dread and dreams die.

Whether you think you can or you think you can't, the chances are you're right!

Over the years, people have asked me how I came to know about banking, export and import, pet insurance, real estate, television, and other ventures. I got into those ventures because I knew I could do it. That mind-set is found within the realm of success. And that's the reason what you think about twenty-four hours a day will determine what you can achieve.

I view my outlook on life as sacred. I do whatever I can to absorb positivity and reject negativity. This means saying no to negative people, negative movies, and anything else that will cloud my thinking or taint my positive outlook. Negative thinking will erode my confidence, and confidence is the goal itself. Self-confidence is my guarantee.

But confidence should not be confused with egotism. Confidence is great unless ego takes over. Ego can make you selfish and arrogant. Self-confidence has enabled me to give speeches in front of thousands of people, but it's not what they think about me that matters so much as what I think about myself. There could be a hundred thousand people, but that doesn't bother me because I believe in what I'm saying. If I believe in my message and I believe in myself, why should I worry about the speech?

Some years ago, while attending a Las Vegas Conference of the American Veterinary Association, an acquaintance of mine stopped me with a sly grin.

"Doctor Jenkins, you're the only black person here with five thousand white people, and you're walking around like you own the place."

That made me laugh. "Why shouldn't I? I'm not afraid of anything, and I like Las Vegas!"

I was in an especially good mood that day because a group of black vets had decided to protest discrimination within the National Veterinary Medical Association. The issues were to be addressed to the executive board in protest of the status of blacks in the association.

MATTHEW JENKINS, DVM

The Chair wishes at this time to recognize a member of the AVMA, Dr. Matthew Jenkins, a practitioner of Compton, Calif., who has a message for the House which, in the opinion of the Chair, will aid in the discussions and deliberations of the House.

Dr. Jenkins, will you please take the microphone at the podium in front of this desk? We ask that you please be somewhat brief in your statements as the House has a pretty heavy schedule and we are running a bit behind time, as per our arrangement.

DR. MATTHEW JENKINS: How much time do I have?

CHAIRMAN TUCKER: Probably 10 or 12 minutes, if that will suffice, Dr. Jenkins.

Black Veterinarians

DR. MATTHEW JENKINS: First, let me say it is an honor to be able to come here today to speak to you gentlemen. I wish to thank Dr. Tucker, Dr. Clarkson, Dr. Price, Dr. Quinn, members of the Executive Board, the delegates from California who have been so kind and who have been so helpful in aiding us in bringing these items we have today to you.

You have a copy of the resolutions. These resolutions have been endorsed by the Southern California Veterinary Medical Association, which is the largest local association in the world. We feel that we could have gotten an endorsement from the state association, if we had time. However, we have talked with these gentlemen, and I have been assured that they will pass on these resolutions in October.

We had about an hour session with the Executive Board on Thursday of this week, and they have also found it necessary to endorse these resolutions. Perhaps I should not read these resolutions—you have them. But, as a result of the meeting with the Executive Board the other day, we have not necessarily an additional resolution but an extension, and this resulted from the many very sincere questions that were asked by the Executive Board. The Executive Board was quite concerned, and they wanted to know why we don't have any more blacks participating in veterinary medicine, why we don't have any more blacks applying to veterinary schools, or why we don't have or, rather, we have fewer veterinarians that are admitted to practice in this country.

So, as a result of this, this addition states that:

". . . the AVMA, deans of veterinary schools, presidents of colleges and many veterinarians are concerned about the small number of minority veterinarians in this country;

". . . an insufficient number of minorities apply to veterinary schools and fewer still are admitted to those schools.

". . . other professional associations have recognized the same problem and have come to grips with it by establishing recruitment programs,"

and as a result of the meeting with the Executive Board, as a result of talks with deans of Tuskegee Institute and other schools, California in particular, we are recommending that: "that AVMA establish a budget for the recruitment of minorities into veterinary schools," this is not necessarily just the Tuskegee Institute, "including, but not limited to advertising in minority publications, participation in various minority seminars, communication with minority junior high schools, minority high schools, and minority colleges."

Now I think, ladies and gentlemen, that, as you look around the room you should look among yourselves and say why is it that I am the only black person in this room? Why? General Snider can tell you, if you were to go to Vietnam right now, you would find a whole lot of black guys there, and they are over there defending all of our rights, and they are defending the right of you to come here and have this meeting.

Blacks want to participate in every form of American society, be it veterinary medicine, be it farming, be it politics, or whatnot. We feel that time is running out with us. We feel that we all should be brothers, that we should be together, that something is wrong when you have 200 or 300 people here representing the hierarchy of veterinary medicine in this country and not one black.

Let's go to the battlefront. We are represented over there in a proportion greater than our population. I say to you that many times you look at the radio, television, the newspaper and you say, "What is the problem?" And I say to you that this is the problem. I say to you that you need blacks on your House of Delegates. I say that you need blacks in your Executive Board. I say that we need blacks in the AVMA office. We need them all the way up to the top and all the way down to the bottom. If we are going to make the mark, I think we have to be fair, and I think it is time for us to stop saying the old adage, "Let George do it." You have the responsibility.

I would like to see this body rise to the occasion of democracy at this time, not next year, not tomorrow, but today.

I would like to see us try and set an example of what we really intend for democracy to be, because the way I have known it, it has

been a farce. I think the young people today are asking questions now. They are saying, "You people have made your living well, let's share. Let's be fair; let's be honest."

If we believe in God, if we believe in the Golden Rule, then I say to you, gentlemen, and I beg of you, I pray with you, please pass these resolutions and the addition, please. Thank you, thank you very much.

At this time the Chair will recognize Dr. Jenkins from California who wishes to make a brief statement to us.

DR. MATTHEW JENKINS: Mr. Chairman, Distinguished Members of the House of Delegates, Members of the Executive Board, Administrative Staff, Members of the Reference Committees: I am real happy to be a member of this organization. I have seen this organization grow substantially in the last seventy-two hours. You have, by your action, translated capricious and arbitrary rhetoric into candid and long-lasting reality.

Although we didn't get all the things through, if for no other reason, we brought to your attention the fact that at a time when there is a critical need for additional veterinarians and additional veterinary schools, we cannot allow any school to die on the vine, whether it be Auburn University, Cornell, University of California at Davis, or Tuskegee Institute. I am hoping that you gentlemen will find it necessary to encourage those individuals, those people that are in positions of authority, to search themselves, to make sure that this fine school at Tuskegee Institute is not allowed to die.

On behalf of Tuskegee Institute, the dean of the veterinary school, Tuskegee Veterinary Alumni, may I say I want to thank you for your consideration. I am real happy. And please remember, let's get more schools; we cannot afford any of them to die. Thank you. [Applause]

Reprint of condensed speeches made at the American Veterinary Medical Convention (AVMA) in Las Vegas in July 1970, which resulted in the dismissal of any state that practices discrimination from membership in the AVMA; placing of blacks in positions of authority throughout the organization; to address itself to the financial needs of those schools in need of financial assistance, including Tuskegee Institute; and to consider the recruitment of minorities at their next meeting.

We had questions, and we wanted answers: "Why is it that no blacks sit on the executive board? Why don't we have more blacks applying to veterinary schools? Why are fewer black veterinarians admitted to practice in this country than whites?"

The black veterinarians encouraged me to take the lead by giving the speech, and I did. I wrote the resolutions alone and then fine-tuned them.

The National Veterinary Association agreed to receive the resolutions and to give us time to air our grievances at the annual convention in Las Vegas in July 1970. It was a hot topic, and that's not just because it was Vegas in July!

I was to present the proclamations, which demanded more diversity in positions of decision-making and outreach to admit more blacks to veterinarian schools and encouragement to practice veterinary medicine.

On the day of my speech, I found myself frantically looking for the black veterinarians to caucus with me before the meeting. I couldn't find them. I ended up presenting the resolutions to the body with a lot of fire and passion, nonetheless. Each resolution was passed, and I received a standing ovation. More importantly, I felt that maybe one day my contribution might add a tiny bit of equality to our country, making America greater country than it had ever been. Every step in the right direction is one step closer to your goal.

Those proclamations turned into laws with the power to dismiss any state organization of the American Veterinary Medical Association found to be engaging in discriminatory practices. Such state organizations could also be dismissed for noncompliance in recruiting minorities. Those laws placed blacks in positions of authority throughout the national organization.

That is an act I am proud to say I spearheaded to bring justice to all segments of American work in veterinary medicine.

When I stood up and the words began to flow, many years of bottled-up intolerance for injustice gushed out of me to reach anyone who was listening.

"I would like to see this body rise to the occasion of democracy! Not tomorrow, not next year, but today!"

I was so proud to speak those words at the House of Delegates of the American Veterinary Medical Association in July 1970.

It was a very good day.

CHAPTER 19

─◦⊰⊱◦─

In the Face of Betrayal

As my veterinary practice grew, I hired two other veterinarians and support staff. Business kept booming, so I hired another veterinarian. He was from out of state, so I paid for his moving expenses.

Three years after that veterinarian began working for me, I decided it was time for a family vacation. We drove down to San Diego that fall, away from everything we knew back home. On our third day, my office manager called. She was fuming.

"Dr. Jenkins, that new doctor quit and opened his own practice."

"Calm down," I told her. "It'll work out."

When I got off the phone, I told Roberta the news.

"What do we do?" Roberta asked.

"Let's go home," I answered.

We packed our bags and returned home to tend to all the clients the doctor had left unattended. He never said a word to me about leaving, and I never asked him about the incident.

A few years later, that doctor's wife called me. He was in the hospital, and she asked me to help her save their practice. I stepped in and tended to his clients. When the doctor got out of the hospital, he asked how much he owed me.

"Nothing," I said.

You can imagine how he felt, both grateful and ashamed of how he'd treated me before. But that wasn't why I did it. He needed help, so I helped him. What did I lose from it? Nothing. The key to keeping a positive mental outlook is to reject negative feelings. Anger is like battery acid eating at the soul and poisoning the mind. Turning away from negative thoughts can be difficult, but it feels good when you do it.

Deciding to reject anger is an intellectual decision. People who say they can't control their emotions are all heart and no head. Be assured that the temptation to embrace anger or other negative feelings is hard to resist. But I have learned to resist anger and keep a cool head when people irritate me. With a cool state of mind, I can channel my energy into active listening and inquiry, which puts me in a position to determine the best way to respond to any difficult situation.

Even now, as an octogenarian, I keep retraining myself to meet such challenges, to recognize them, and aspire to overcome any difficulty in my pursuits. You reap what you sow, as the saying goes, and that's especially meaningful to someone who grew up on a farm.

Positive thought brings positive rewards.

For example, if you respect your employees and they know you value them and expect a lot from them, what you'll get back in return is a job well done. Employers must hold themselves to the same high standards they have for their employees if they expect to make a positive impact in the workplace.

For example, my mother expected extremely hard work from her employees, and they never resisted her because she worked as hard in the fields and the business as they did.

Once you have assured employees that they can expect fairness from you, you develop an atmosphere of trust. When the boss treats employees with respect, it is more likely those employees will treat that business the same way. If a boss treats employees poorly, he or she can expect that employee to repay the company in kind. And that can be the difference between profit and loss. Whether the business is struggling or thriving, what goes around comes around.

I've often had people tell me, "You go overboard for your employees. You pay them far too much."

What they fail to understand is that if employees know their boss is understanding of their needs and goes overboard to create a positive work atmosphere, those employees will be loyal.

Years ago, while serving on the Board of Trustees at Claremont Graduate University in Claremont, California, I had the opportunity to interact with the great Peter Drucker. He is considered a foundational figure in ethical management, publishing more than thirty books on business principles. Drucker wrote about every feature of the modern economy, but a common thread constantly ran through his writings: humanitarian values.

When an employer creates a trusting and respectful atmosphere, it engenders employee loyalty. This is true in your family, in your community, and in your business. It always comes back to values. If you value others, they will value you. If you smile at the world, the world will smile back at you, even if it sometimes takes a while.

In business, customers are your greatest advertisers. If you treat them right, they will recommend you to others. This seems elementary, but too many business owners forget this. The customer may not always be right, but they should always be treated right. You can't have angry customers talking badly about you. It will destroy your business.

One thing I learned early in my practice and something which I couldn't seem to get other doctors to understand, it pays to give a little extra to customers. I gave away a lot of medicine. People would come in, and if a treatment wasn't working quite right, I would find ways to do something for their pet free of charge. When an animal was ready to go home after a stay in the hospital, I'd give it a bath at no charge. The next day, I would call the client to see how the animal was doing. I found that giving to customers brought in more business.

By valuing my clients, I generated a positive reputation, and that's really how my practice grew. People would bring their pets to me from thirty-five southern California cities; I had people flying in from as far away as San Francisco.

Commonly heard among my customers was "Dr. Jenkins got the touch."

I stuck to my "seven days a week for seven years" game plan and grew my practice. That foundation of diligence, hard work, good practices, and targeted growth enabled me to retire at the age of forty-five, exactly as I had planned back in college. After I accomplished that goal, I sold my practice to other Tuskegee veterinarian graduates who had been on our staff for several years—Drs. John Evans and Emanuel Grain. Then I moved to my next full-time career in real estate.

⬥⚬⚬⬥

That segment of my life marked the closing of one chapter and the opening of another—entrepreneurial investment. My years in veterinary medicine, real-estate investment, banking, and other ventures were all part of the larger legacy left by my father and mother.

By that time in my career, I understood that entrepreneurial leaders share a common trait: they work harder and smarter than the competition. Talent without effort is wasted time, but talent coupled with a strong work ethic is a recipe for success.

One of the keys to success in your life's purpose is to establish long-term goals and measure the results of every effort along the way. I would never have chosen to go to Greenland, but I followed my oath. And as a veterinarian, I knew that solving a major rabies outbreak would bode well for me later and make a positive impact on the lives of many people and animals.

People often attribute talent to success, but the most successful in any field are almost always usually the hardest workers and the most dedicated. Michael Jordan and Kobe Bryant made basketball look easy because they spent tens of thousands of hours refining their skills. Steve Jobs and Steve Wozniak have been called prodigies and they were, but they also put in the time and hard work necessary to achieve incredible success.

Scientists have found that one-third of what we become is part of our DNA, while the other two-thirds come from our environment, and by environment, I mean parenting, training, and socialization.

I think there are instances in which our genetic components may include unhealthy characteristics from previous generations that we know nothing about. Obviously, everyone would like to win the lottery with great genes, but we all know more than one person who had great potential but didn't reach his or her potential. In poker, those who are dealt great cards but play them poorly will lose to those who are dealt average cards, but play them well. The will and my game plan offer important features for success.

When I was methodically building my real-estate portfolio and reached a planned milestone, I would reward myself with a trip to another country that I had always wanted to see. In the '70s, one gainful milestone took me to China.

President Nixon had just begun the People-to-People Program between the United States and China. Roberta and I joined a group of veterinarians who took advantage of the program to visit farms, veterinary schools, factories, the Great Wall, and other sites. Travel between China and the United States had been restricted for about two decades, so most Chinese people had never seen anyone except other Chinese. When we came out of our hotel taking photographs, nearly a hundred Chinese surrounded us.

"Ali, Ali," they chanted, walking right up close and almost touching us. I had to smile when they spied me in our group, a six foot four black man, believing me to be the famous fighter.

Roberta took a picture of me in the middle of all those boxing fans with our Polaroid camera, which was almost as amazing to them as meeting the heavyweight champion of the world. Most Chinese had never seen an instant photo of themselves, and since I was Ali, they all wanted a photo with me. When she pulled the photos from the camera and handed them out, most of them held it close to their chest, bowing in gratitude.

I concluded that no matter how hard the Chinese government had fought to keep outside information from its people, somehow, Muhammad Ali managed to slip through the cracks. Excellence always finds its way past resistance.

CHAPTER 20

⊰❈⊱

My Second Career in Real Estate

My current house in Long Beach is a just few steps from the beach, overlooking the beautiful Pacific Ocean. On a clear day, I can see Catalina and the San Clemente Islands on the horizon. During our time here, Roberta and I have thrown some great parties and fund-raisers. It's hard to believe that nobody wanted to buy our oceanfront home for three years before we came along.

Maybe it stayed vacant for such a long time because the property was previously owned by Vivian Laird Hill, Bugsy Siegel's girl-friend. Her initials were still emblazoned on the downstairs shower door in 1978. Or maybe it was vacant longer than usual because the primary flat adjoined an unconventional configuration of condominiums with shared garages. Whatever the reason, none of that bothered us. Both Roberta and I loved the view of the ocean and could envision what the shuttered home built inside the hill adjoining the oceanfront could look like with a little tender loving care. I mentally calculated the value of the place after remodeling as we toured the property.

Five minutes after that first walk through, I said to the agent, "We'll take it."

The agent looked shocked when I pulled out documents and started drafting the agreement. After three years with no takers, I figured our offer would be accepted, and it was.

142

I saw *positive possibilities* in that large parcel of land with ocean-front views, only a short drive to downtown Long Beach. But there's more to the story. In the years prior to purchasing that property, I learned to buy properties around the country sight unseen. So while it seemed fast to the agent, spending five minutes on that home site was like a lifetime to me.

I had become an expert at purchasing properties sight unseen because I knew some property owners would not sell to me because of my race and banks wouldn't lend to me for the same reason. This racist reality existed in all parts of the country but fully manifested itself in the Deep South. In other parts of the country, racism showed up in more subtle ways. It was a cancer over which I had little or no control, so I devised my game plan to win, regardless. No matter the obstacles, no matter who tried to block my game plan, I always moved forward.

My game plan to deal with that challenge was to use the wisdom passed down to me from my parents—never blow up and allow racism to defeat you.

I planned to outsmart racism doing just that.

I learned how to research properties and write good contracts. Over time, I developed a method for acquiring pictures, financial and tax records, and statistics on occupancies and vacancies, along with information about amenities such as clubhouses, swimming pools, and tennis courts. I would review ongoing expenses such as water and gas rates. Then I factored the information into a cost-benefit analysis to determine if I should invest. Whether it was a property worth a hundred thousand dollars or five million, the formula remained the same. If I erred, it was on the side of being too thorough.

Armed with my research and contractual knowledge, I could make a profitable real-estate purchase from even the bitterest racist. I would write a contract and send it to the potential seller. Once the property owner signed the contract, it was legally binding. If the physical inspection uncovered major problems or other concerns, I held a signed agreement that gave me the legal right to back out of the contract.

Therein lay my advantage. I had written contingencies into the contracts to guard against a forced purchase or the loss of my deposit. Throughout my life, I have found that it is possible to gain tremendous leverage by virtue of understanding all possible legal channels and then making the most strategic decisions possible. Getting angry at injustice is foolish. Better to be prepared. I felt that I had to take what was equitable by my own intelligence and devices and by finding the boldness to stand up for what was written and signed.

Winning prizefighters know it's best to control anger, keep your composure, and stay focused on the competition. One can only overcome injustice with calm calculation. Anger and its toxic cousins cloud the mind and lead to failure. Injustice is inevitable; as are difficult and hateful people.

A good game plan wins every time.

Doing business often means dealing with people who might not like you. But all relationships are voluntary, which means you don't have control over anyone else. People may hate me because I'm black, or not black enough, or too tall, or not tall enough. I don't have any control over that. So I have to protect my interests by diligent planning and attention to detail.

The primary determinant of success are your goals and the corresponding game plan to reach them. If I want to buy some property and I know certain people will not sell to me, how can I overcome that? I would thoroughly research the property. I would put all of that data together and come up with a reasonable price. I'd give myself a margin of safety, factoring in a financial buffer—up to twenty percent on my initial offer. I may overlook an ongoing expense, but if I add a cushion as my margin of safety, I'll still be okay. The devil is in the details, as they say, but proper preparation is the angel on your shoulder.

I also execute that formula for stress-free travel. If I'm driving to Los Angeles and it should take me twenty minutes, I might leave thirty minutes before my appointment. Traffic may get tough, but if I build in a margin of time above what I need, I will usually arrive on time.

Time management is one of the most undervalued skills in both personal and professional situations. I'm an ardent believer in getting the job done on time, but I also advocate establishing realistic and a sustainable game plan to make it happen.

A vital key for any entrepreneur is to concentrate energy in the places that produce the best results. There's no point in wasting energy on futility. Channel your energy toward *positive possibilities*.

Ask yourself: what is the best solution to resolve this challenge? Then work the solution.

Paul Williams is considered one of the most iconic Los Angeles architects. In his lifetime, he designed hundreds of homes for movie stars, including Frank Sinatra and many other celebrities. He also designed many famous commercial buildings, such as the space-age-themed building I see every time I fly in and out of Los Angeles International Airport.

Williams worked twice as hard as most architects to etch his legacy into Angelino history. He learned to draw blueprints upside down so prospective clients on the other side of the table could watch him create designs of buildings the client had just described.

Williams earned a reputation as a no nonsense professional who completed projects rapidly, sometimes overnight. As the first black architect accepted into the American Institute of Architecture, Williams surely faced his share of prejudice, but he didn't let other people define his success. His game plan outworked and outcompeted the competition.

There's no point becoming apathetic in the face of injustice or any other disadvantage. If you realize the odds are stacked against you, focus all your mental and physical energy on finding the next *positive possibility*. Learn everything you can, and with a cool head, figure out a winning game plan.

Take the Los Angeles Lakers. If they're playing a fast-moving team like Oklahoma City, they'll try to slow things down. If they're playing a team that is methodical and like Chicago, they might employ a lot of fast breaks. Look at each of life's situations from your best vantage point and craft your game plan to win.

You may have three, or four, or five professions during a lifetime, so it's critical to never stop learning. That's the reason I took surgery classes at UCLA and, later, real-estate classes, even while I was busy with my veterinary practice. Reading is an important key to unlocking the world and opening many doors. Learn to discipline yourself to read instead of watching television. I read because it inspires me, often ushering me into a state of comfort and tranquility, and it can do the same for you.

CHAPTER 21

─────◦⟨⟩◦─────

Botched Deal Pays Off

One thing is certain about a real-estate investment career: setbacks come with the process. As my veterinary practice grew, Roberta and I bought our first little investment properties—two single-family rental homes in Compton. Later, we purchased a forty-unit apartment building in Los Angeles and forty acres of land in Riverside, California.

Our next investment was triggered by a chance meeting. Roberta met a group of women through a friend, all wives of professionals—dentists, physicians, lawyers, and veterinarians. Over time, I became friends with Roberta's friends and their spouses, and we all had a lot of fun together.

During a gathering at our house, we discussed what we felt was most needed in the Compton community. We agreed that a first-rate motel with tennis courts, a swimming pool, and meeting rooms would greatly improve Compton's economic viability and create an upscale image.

Holiday Inn was just beginning to roll out in our area, and several members of our group agreed that the prospect was worth considering. I contacted the company's franchise office and learned the company's criteria for selecting new locations was simple: a large plot of land near a large city on a heavily traveled street. That narrowed the scope of our property search.

The next task was to identify a real-estate agent. A few days later, while driving from an emergency call at seven o'clock in the morning, I noticed a real-estate sign adjacent to a mobile home park. I jotted the number down and called to inquire about available land for sale that met the criteria for a Holiday Inn franchise. The real-estate agent asked where I had gotten his name, and I told him I had seen the sign next to the mobile home park.

He immediately said, "Why don't you buy that park?"

"It has homes on it," I answered.

"That's no problem," he said. "According to California law, all you have to do is give them a thirty-day notice to move and you have your land."

The agent made a convincing case, and the land met all of Holiday Inn's requirements; it sat on a major avenue, adjacent to the Long Beach (I-710) Freeway. I researched the related real-estate laws and confirmed that it would be easy to convert the land use from a mobile home park to a motel. I met with the partners and discussed the plan: each of us would invest ten thousand dollars, giving us the eighty thousand dollars we needed to make the offer for the Holiday Inn franchise. The partners told me to put the property in escrow and they would put their money in later. I put five thousand dollars down to move the property into escrow.

What happened next stunned me: every one of my prospective partners declined on their investment commitment. I called the real-estate agent and asked for my five thousand dollars deposit back. I was stunned again when he refused, because according to California law, he had fulfilled the listing requirement and did not have to return the deposit. He followed up the bad news with an interesting proposition.

"Doctor Jenkins, buy this property. It could be your retirement."

That night, I discussed the matter with Roberta. "We're young," I said. "Just getting started. If we're going to make a bad decision, let's make it while we're still young. That way, we have time to recover."

Roberta agreed.

My wife always offered support while also raising concerns. She was much more cautious than me. I would pull her along while she kept me from going too fast—the yin and yang. If I had been six-ty-five years old, I probably would not have purchased that property because I would not have had much longer in the workforce. But back then, the decision felt right.

I worked out a deal with the seller, who wanted to hold the note so he could have monthly income. He took the note back on the permanent loan. I put a total of twenty thousand dollars down, which included my initial five-thousand-dollar deposit, another five thousand dollars in cash, and a ten-thousand-dollar loan from my bank. I moved forward because I wanted to start my real-estate port-folio. The rest is history.

In our first month of ownership, the park netted $682 after all expenses. Still, I proceeded with plans to clear the mobile home park to make way for a motel development. But with each passing month, I became increasingly interested in the mobile home park business.

I would call the onsite property manager to check in. "How are things going?"

"Fine."

"Any vacancies?"

"No."

"Anyone late on rent?"

"No."

Month after month, I realized how much easier and more prof-itable the mobile park was to operate than the forty-unit apartment building in Los Angeles. We experienced a whole slate of problems with the tenants renting our apartments and houses.

The positive trend at the mobile home park continued. Eventually, the opportunity became clear to me, and I told Roberta that we needed to get rid of our apartment building and housing rentals and get more mobile home parks.

Soon, the botched motel investment was a distant memory. Those would-be investors, who failed to follow through on their monetary commitments, never asked me about that investment or any of my subsequent ventures. The whole experience taught me to check people's deeds, not their words. All too often, business dealings with friends go awry because of informality. I have found that contracts are essential in establishing expectations and commitments.

Overall, I feel eminently fortunate to have unwittingly discovered the mobile home park investment opportunity. To me, it was another truth of the power of *positive possibilities*. Betrayals and failed business ventures can be looked upon as endings or opportunities for new beginnings.

Prize-winning sociologist Sara Lawrence-Lightfoot explores this concept in her book *Exit: The Endings That Set Us Free*. Had I bemoaned the collapse of the motel development, I might have closed my eyes to the tremendous investment possibility that lay before me.

Roberta and I were having problems with our rentals, and then this mobile home park fell into our laps and opened our eyes to a whole new investment possibility that ended up changing our lives. The park had onsite management, so all Roberta and I had to do was pick up the rent money each month. I didn't know much about the mobile home park business, but I soon realized that it offered low maintenance and great profitability.

I decided to change my game plan.

I proceeded with plans to remodel the mobile home park. To maximize profitability, I developed the vacant land included in the purchase and converted it into new lots. I also established standard maintenance procedures for homeowners, which elevated the culture in the park. I knew that proud homeowners meant a positive community and good business. To encourage pride of ownership, I gave "Yard of the Month" awards, which came with one month's free rent. Occasionally, I'd have to fine or evict an odd scofflaw tenant or two, but overall, I was very pleased with my first mobile home park investment.

Talk to any successful entrepreneur, and they will tell you there will be situations where it is necessary to regroup, to adapt and innovate in response to unexpected scenarios.

In other words, if game plan A isn't working, develop game plan B. When we purchased that forty-unit apartment building, we didn't expect it to be such a headache. People wouldn't pay their rent, tenants gave us legal troubles, and vacancy rates were too high. This was typical of the culture of people who rent apartments in lower socio-economic settings. Making matters doubly difficult was the reality that the laws favored tenants above owners. Conversely, mobile home parks were far easier to deal with from an investment and management standpoint. The owner owns the land and tenants own their homes. If tenants don't follow the rental policies, management can evict them. That seemed equitable to me.

With those facts in hand, we drew one conclusion: we needed to unload our forty-unit apartment building. We put it up for sale, but nobody wanted to buy it. So we considered other options and learned about a federal program that offered tax rebates for donating properties to charities.

I researched the program and discovered that if I donated our apartment building to a church, I would get four installments of $25,000 over a four-year period, plus tax considerations on other income. I used those $25,000 installments to make down payments on two other mobile home parks. The second park I bought was originally valued at $250,000. I put down $25,000 on the park and then offered rental discounts to bring it to full occupancy. That property now is worth about four million dollars.

The following year, we used the next $25,000 we got from the government to purchase a third park in San Bernardino. I later sold that property for more than $1.2 million.

Successful investment requires careful analysis of both performing and nonperforming assets. I determined that mobile home parks were performing well, whereas our forty-unit apartment building was not. By utilizing a government tax program, I was able to help a local church while transitioning my assets into a more promising direction. Roberta and I came out ahead because we were able to use those tax rebate funds to purchase more lucrative real-estate holdings. I found that by learning every possible legal and financial option, I was able to make the most strategic decision.

This is why it is critical to remain updated on new laws enacted in any profession—tax laws, real-estate laws, and any other legal entity or organization that affects your business. It's the same logic as in sports: if a rule is changed, coaches and athletes should consider the opportunities and challenges posed by the modification to be sure they maintain their competitive edge. It turned out that my game plan B worked better than my game plan A. That is the formula I used to overcome every one of my most challenging circumstances.

That's how I did everything. I conceptualized every aspect of my life within the context of seeking *positive possibilities* and master game planning. That forty-unit apartment was worth more than the one hundred thousand dollars we received for donating it, but it still made sense to unload it.

Why? Because it was a drag on our overall real-estate portfolio. By cutting our losses on that building, we could parlay the tax benefit into more promising investments to continue to grow our business.

In those years, however, mobile home parks carried a negative stigma, so many investors shied away from them. I learned as a young boy with those baby bulls we bought for a dollar each, that great opportunities are often found in areas that others ignore or under-value. Just as I raised those overlooked baby bulls into full-grown cattle we sold for handsome profits, I saw great potential in mobile home parks. At that time, it was the center of my future growth and profitability.

CHAPTER 22

⌐◦⊰§⊱◦⌐

Growth in an Unknown Market

With my first three mobile home parks in southern California already profitable, I turned my attention to out-of-state opportunities. My rationale was simple: California was a bellwether for the rest of the country. Over the years, I had observed that national trends start in California and then head east.

I carefully analyzed market trends and established my most ambitious game plan to date. I determined that the mobile home park industry offered one of the best hedges against inflation, a major economic concern. In the mobile or manufactured housing business, it was possible to raise rents annually to accommodate cost-of-living increases. However, due to low maintenance, the increase in annual operating expenses go up very little, making it possible to actually increase my income even during high inflationary times. My own research was consistent with articles published in such periodicals as the *Wall Street Journal* and the *Los Angeles Times*.

I continued to review my options and financial possibilities. Our three southern California mobile home parks were realizing a cash-on-cash invested return, running about fifty percent. The risks Roberta and I had taken by acquiring that first mobile home park in the face of the botched motel deal shed light on an incredible national opportunity.

Knowing that many people could not afford to buy conventional housing, I began searching for undervalued mobile home parks in other states—Virginia, North Carolina, South Carolina, Georgia, Ohio, Indiana, Alabama, and Louisiana. I had bold plans.

I formed a limited partnership and recruited investors to buy shares in some of our mobile home park ventures. All my market research and projections led me to one conclusion: an investment boom was on the horizon. I used our first two parks to secure a line of credit to purchase a mobile home park in Indiana for $1.8 million. I negotiated a twenty-five to thirty percent discount on the property because I bought the park outright using my line of credit.

I immediately borrowed two hundred thousand dollars to refurbish and market the newly acquired park. Once I brought the park up to greatly improved occupancy, I secured a conventional loan to pay off my line of credit. That method of financing enabled me to add another profitable property to my real-estate portfolio without using a penny of my own cash. After taking monthly profits from that park for several years, we finally sold it for four million dollars. In essence, I developed a targeted game plan for manufactured homes that paid big dividends. At our peak, we owned eighteen parks in eight different states.

My analysis of the manufactured home sector proved correct, but identifying the investment opportunity was just the first step. For our investments to prosper, we needed to outcompete the competition. So I came up with the game plan to reach that goal.

I knew that mobile home parks carried a stigma of blight and crime. To aggressively challenge that assumption, I would give each of our new parks a series of upgrades, which brought loyalty from existing tenants. I began to offer six months free rent to new tenants, meaning that they would pay half of their rent for twelve months. That promotion quickly pushed our parks to maximum occupancy.

I sought to maximize profits by finding ways to expand the parks. In North Carolina, we expanded our park from 400 to 500 units; in Virginia, we grew our park from 500 to 637. Those promotional discounts and expansion efforts allowed our parks to rapidly reach maximum capacity and profitability.

The pools at Country Manor Estates mobile home park near Mooresville have undergone renovations worth $55,000.

Rich Miller/The Indianapolis News

New owner and managers spark renaissance in mobile home park

By LESLEY S. STEDMAN
The Indianapolis News

MOORESVILLE, Ind. — More than just the name of Lantern Hills Mobile Home Park changed when a Long Beach, Calif., businessman bought the Mooresville area property two years ago.

Matthew Jenkins, owner of 12 other parks across the nation, poured more than $500,000 into the park and renamed it Country Manor Estates. He had roads paved, security lights installed, trees planted and the clubhouse renovated.

An additional $55,000 was dedicated to improving the swimming pools. The park pond was enlarged, cleaned and restocked — twice.

But, according to residents, Jenkins' best move was hiring two new managers, Vernon and Joyce Mitchell.

When the Mitchells, each in their early 50s, took over the property in April of 1989, weeds had overgrown the pond, the buildings were in shambles, the roads were full of potholes and violence threatened the residents.

"Before the changes, Morgan County and state police (practically) lived in this area 'cause of the stuff going on," said 10-year resident Barbara Young. "You couldn't walk anywhere because you were afraid you'd get attacked by a dog or some kid."

When the Mitchells took over, they concentrated on evicting tenents who experienced domestic violence, abused drugs and alcohol and failed to maintain their lots.

Californian
bought park
2 years ago

— Matthew Jenkins

"We're getting in a new class of people," Joyce Mitchell said of the park population, which has grown from fewer than 200 homes to more than 400 in the two years. "These are nice people with good jobs.

"They started mowing their lawns, planting gardens, building decks and just making the place look better almost right away," she said, pointing out some of the yard-of-the-month homes.

But the people of Country Manor appreciate more than just a safer, cleaner neighborhood.

It is the big hearts of the spunky managers that has impressed residents, who day in and day out see the two put in 14 or 15 hour days. Living on the property, the Mitchells are open to phone calls all night, often interrupting their sleep to help their neighbors.

The Mitchells have also been known to help tenants out financially. Young re-

members when they loaned money and bought new clothes for needy children.

"No child will go hungry in this neighborhood if she knows about it," said Young, thumbing toward her landlady.

The kids are the Mitchells' biggest concern.

"You know, I worry about those young ones, playing outside and all," Joyce Mitchell said. "I love 'em all. We're a community, a family."

Although the park's curfew is 9:30 p.m., the couple often stays in the office late to allow a group of boys to play basketball or swim in the pool after hours.

The Mitchells also helped create a teenage club that meets one Thursday each month.

"We had a get-out-of-school party that was great," said an enthusiastic Terry Smith, 15. "There was music, pop, chips, hotdogs, all in the clubhouse. It was really fun."

Living at the park for 2½ years, Smith has witnessed many of the changes. He's excited by the increase in the number of kids his age, especially since "no one's runnin' wild anymore."

The Mitchells' work has more than satisfied their boss.

"I wanted to create a nice facility that people could be proud of," said Jenkins, who has raised rent $10, making a lot $150 per month. "People take care of what they're proud of.

"And that's what the Mitchells have been able to provide — good living."

155

To push the notion that I was offering a quality product, I referred to the units in our parks as "manufactured homes" rather than mobile homes or trailers. Yet rebranding the parks was more than wordplay. Residents at every one of our parks experienced significant quality-of-life improvements.

The Indianapolis News noted that, after purchasing the Lantern Hills Mobile Home Park, I renamed it Country Manor Estates, but they also observed that beyond a name upgrade, residents benefited from more than five hundred thousand dollars in upgrades. The newspaper wrote: "*Roads were paved, security lights installed, trees planted, and the clubhouse renovated.*" They added, "*He renovated the swimming pools and cleaned and expanded the park's pond, twice stocking it with fish.*"

During the height of that positive swell, I advertised in the *Wall Street Journal* that I was seeking to purchase manufactured home parks around the country. In localities where I owned parks, I would advertise vacancies and promotions on billboards. In some cases, I would arrange private deals with landowners who lived beside major highways. I would pay a monthly fee for them to put up my billboards. I also leased billboards on land I owned to create new revenue streams. For years, a CBS affiliate leased billboard space I owned along the 710 Freeway in Compton, adjacent to my first manufactured home park.

With a superior housing product and targeted advertising and promotion, my investments in the manufactured home sector boomed. Still, some people would caution me about the social stigma of investing in housing for those earning lower incomes.

I rejected that attitude for several reasons. To begin with, I don't waste my time on stigmas and stereotypes. Second, I didn't intend to perpetuate the status quo in the manufactured home business. I planned to trump the competition by offering a superior housing product. I sought to grow investments while also giving people with modest to mid-level incomes the opportunity to live in a safe and healthy environment.

People who are blinded by stigmas and stereotypes fail to see many opportunities. Again and again, I returned to the power of *positive possibilities*, seeking to derive positive outcome from every situation. Had Roberta and I remained focused on maintaining our nonperforming forty-unit apartment building, we would have limited our possibilities. Had we bought into the stigma about mobile home parks rather than making them better, we would have missed out on one of our best investment opportunities. Most of those who invested with us on those ventures enjoyed handsome returns.

From a business standpoint, it is important to evaluate investments from a long-term perspective, looking at each asset's financial and tax considerations. If an investment is underperforming, consider taking a loss on it or giving it to charity. Doing so often enables you to offset taxes from other tax producing assets you may have. We donated that apartment building and a few houses for that reason. We've also donated land in Virginia, Georgia, and Alabama.

We have the property appraised and then determine the amount we can deduct from our income-producing operations. If it makes good financial sense, that's what we do. I lecture at various schools on this approach.

Pomona College, which is part of the Claremont University Consortium, was a pioneer in receiving donated property for tax offsets. That's the reason Pomona College has one of the highest endowments per capita of any school in the United States.

Successful investors know when to cut their losses and when to take profits.

I owned some manufactured home parks that dropped in occupancy after a nearby military base closed, but that's just ordinary business. You never know what's going to happen.

To adapt to that unexpected development, I inventoried all assets associated with those properties. The undeveloped land on those properties was lush with big pine trees. I drew on my childhood farm experience dealing with timber and initiated a plan to harvest and sell that timber, which proved profitable. I then consolidated the properties and eventually sold everything for a modest profit.

It wasn't what I had hoped for from the outset, but I maximized my profits via the timber sale and was soon free and clear of a nonperforming asset. As I said, you never know what's going to happen.

We had another manufactured home park in Virginia, twenty-nine acres right on the water, and a hurricane took it!

What do you do?

You seek the *positive possibilities* and get a new game plan. The good news was that homeowner's insurance held by each tenant covered the loss of the 150 homes destroyed in the hurricane, which meant we were not liable for those costs. In the months ahead, local authorities established new regulations on coastal homes requiring stilt construction, which was considerably more expensive.

Those new regulations made it impossible to rebuild manufactured homes on the coastal site, but fortunately, the property was paid for, and we had a good reserve. So we closed everything and held onto the property for seven years until we finally auctioned it off. We made a decent profit, although not the money you would normally make on a situation like that. But we minimized our losses and sold at a prudent time.

I cannot state the importance of calculating value in conjunction with evaluating the marketplace timing of a given investment. In other words, some properties were worth keeping because they could become a valuable future asset. We held on to our farmland because we anticipated that it would have strong development potential for commercial and residential purposes in the future. Ignoring marketplace timing could mean selling a property for a tenth of what it might be worth in a few years.

CHAPTER 23

❖❖❖

Managing a Diversified Enterprise

The second phase of my career in real-estate investment was booming, but I knew that maintaining that success would require vigilance and innovation in response to inevitable changes in the global economy. During that time, my research confirmed that most American millionaires made their money in real estate. But I wasn't about to become complacent with my portfolio.

I kept current by reading and doing research, knowing that real estate might not always be the most prudent investment. I was a "read-a-holic" of in-depth information related to my investments and interests. I kept active files on all my holdings.

I recommend that before making an official move toward change and take the time to gather the facts and the know-how. If you don't know how, stop and learn how. Every project requires the correct tools, skills, and facts. Make sure all facts are indeed facts and trends gathered from reliable sources too, such as the *Wall Street Journal*.

Eliminate bogus information and ignore stigmas, stereotypes, and propaganda that muddy accurate perceptions. Once you have the knowledge and know-how edge, proceed with confidence and diligence. Don't pay attention to the naysayers. The doctors who agreed to invest in my first real-estate mobile home park doubted my investment abilities because they saw me as a doctor with only

159

medical knowledge, just like them. But they hadn't taken the investment courses I had taken. They didn't read the *Wall Street Journal* every day.

Those were the tools that helped me decide how to identify and reject bad opportunities. From such credible information, I could buy profitable real estate, including four farms in Alabama and a wind farm in northern California we own with my brother, Levaughn. We own the land and rent to wind farmers in northern California and crop farmers in Alabama.

At one point, I tried my hand in the import/export business. We were shipping products to Nigeria, which I felt served an important need; but collecting payments for goods delivered proved to be challenging beyond all tolerance. After assessing the long-term prospects of our new business, we decided to shut it down. We took a loss on our taxes and moved on.

The key to running any diversified investment portfolio is to be sure your businesses are working for you and not dragging you down. Saying yes to a lemon could mean saying no to the next great investment opportunity.

As I said earlier, even the best homerun hitters strike out. Tepid success with the import/export business proved a good learning experience. I didn't let it cloud my confidence in future ventures.

If you've done your research and analysis, you can afford to be bold. That's why I have invested in different sectors of the economy. In 1970, I diversified into cable television stations. The venture held great potential, but it was not without difficulties.

We built our first station in Charleston, South Carolina, and later acquired a license to launch a station in Las Vegas. As months passed, I learned that the general manager running the station in South Carolina was dishonest. I received reports that he was addicted to cocaine and the company was not repaying money I had loaned it. That situation proved challenging, to say the least. After finally retrieving the money I had loaned the station, I decided that was it for me with television. We sold the South Carolina station and the Las Vegas license in a wash and moved on.

Looking back, it's clear we should have sold that station for a higher price. Had we held on to the South Carolina station and launched the one in Las Vegas, we would have profited from the boom in cable television in the years ahead, just as CNN did when it went on the air about the same time.

You win some, you lose some; the key is to keep adapting. Years later, I saw considerable opportunity in a technology company that develops software for replacing body parts—knees, hips, and spines. In fact, they'll probably be sending me a check soon. With investing, timing is everything. If you don't have a long-term game plan for a given asset, you may sell at the wrong time and lose.

Investment is all about research, imagination, strategic planning, and timing. As you've seen, I've explored opportunities in a broad range of economic sectors. But regardless of the sector, one element most determines a company's success: honesty.

The biggest problem I've had dealing with companies I'm not in charge of is the honesty factor—the fairness factor. I end up being the moral conscience of the company because I always want to do things the right way and be honest with investors and customers. I find this notion of being fair and honest is foreign to a lot of people. Now I'm convinced that if you enter business just to make money, you will never make enough of it, but if you go into business with values of fairness and honesty, your success will reflect that.

In 1978, I began to serve as the chairman of the board of the Bank of Finance. That was when my good friend and moral ally, Los Angeles Mayor Tom Bradley, was on the board. I found that a lot of board members thought the bank was their personal piggy bank. I believed we owed it to the investors to be aboveboard with everything, and never, under any circumstances, take advantage of our position as board members.

For those reasons, I established a policy requiring anyone on the board who was seeking a personal loan to apply at our corresponding bank, meaning the parent bank would service the applicant. This avoided obvious conflicts of interest and proved to be the best practice advocated by the Federal Deposit Insurance Corporation (FDIC). It was a matter of strongly promoting a wholesome leadership culture, which meant no deviation from moral and ethical practices.

I've had connections to business dealings where others went to prison, but I never did.

I didn't because I made instantaneous decisions based on honor and integrity, which I didn't even realize was such a deep part of me at that time. One instance involved the mayor of a fairly large city. In one of our conversations, he made an uncanny statement.

"Since you've got property in various states, we should get together and talk sometime. I think you can help us and we can help you."

Intrigued by the mutually beneficial opportunity, I met with that mayor, two city councilmen, and two real-estate agents.

The mayor opened the discussion. "We've got this land on the water, and we can take it out of redevelopment agency holdings," he said. "I'll pay redevelopment a dollar an acre for it, and then we can develop it into condos and make a lot of money."

I didn't have to think about it one minute. My moral barometer flared. "That's illegal," I said.

"No, no. Our attorneys have checked it out, and they say it's legal."

"Count me out," I said.

Now that's an instantaneous decision based solely on my value system. My integrity and honesty are things you can't just put on a shelf. They must be deeply ingrained in you. I know too many people who have gone down an unethical path because they were convinced that a particular action was legal. Legality can be highly subjective. Many things are legal but not right. As my mother said, "There's no right way to do wrong." I've followed her lead my entire life.

When I give talks to young people, I challenge them to imagine that everything they do will be front-page news. Then I push them to consider if that front-page news makes them proud or embarrassed. If you're happy with what you envision, you'll probably make a good decision. If you're disappointed or concerned, you need to stop in your tracks because greedy intentions are obvious and usually turn out badly. So when the politicians tried to entice me into that shady real-estate deal, they met with my value system, and I was out of there. The FBI threw the book at them, and they went to prison.

I have found that if you train yourself to engage each moment seeking *positive possibilities*, you will wake up in the morning with a sense of freedom, living the highest standards in everything you do.

Most people who get busted for big crimes are doomed not by that crime but rather a series of minor offenses and decisions driven by tainted values. The big crime might have been what got them locked up, but it was the petty crimes and unethical acts they committed beforehand that lead them there. Those smaller things overwhelmed their good values.

Corruption is a slippery slope. You steal one hundred dollars and get away with it. No big deal? Wrong. It ruins your values and your life. Such ruin doesn't happen in a vacuum. In the long term, decide to do right and never regret it. You may not always get the results you are seeking, but you can always be proud of your actions.

CHAPTER 24

⟡

Listening and Learning to Eliminate Delusions

I've found that to succeed long term in anything, it's critical to be totally honest with yourself. Such honesty requires paying close attention to the observations of other people you respect and trust. Those are the people who will tell you the truth and not what you want to hear. These trusted people may not always be right, but they will raise observations and perspectives that are invaluable. Even the best of us can lose perspective now and then.

Paying close attention to such inner-circle advisors ensures that you will factor in unconsidered perspectives while you work to promote clarity and veracity to operate your business to profitability.

For my business corporation, SDD Enterprises, Inc., I have a board of directors, and I always encourage them to tell me their honest opinions, and I extend them the same courtesy. I seek to establish a culture of honesty and respect, even in times when my thoughts are diametrically opposed to other members on the board. The best thing for the company to do is to bring everybody's ideas to the table. Then we figure out the best way to proceed as a group, based on the collective facts we have to work with.

In 1986, Reagan's tax reform law took a lot of the incentives out of buying property. I had been out buying and buying and buying! I was completely focused on growing the enterprise. But the board members recommended that I stop buying properties. I considered their recommendations and asked what we would do with all the money. The consensus was that we should pay off all our debts.

I'll be honest; I was enjoying buying all those properties. Investments were booming, and I wanted to keep buying. But I reflected and ultimately saw the board members' wisdom. So I stopped buying, and it was the best thing I could have ever done. Interest rates shot up to as high as 22%, which meant we paid off our notes and eliminated debt before that high interest rate hit our payments. Had I ignored the wisdom of my board, I would have lost big time.

The bottom line is that employers get delusional when they validate and reinforce their own thinking in a vacuum of "yes" people.

Trusted advisors offer essential checks and balances. In management and all other aspects of business, each person needs checks and balances all the way up and down the chain of command to make sure that the person at the bottom can talk to top personnel in special circumstances. If such a system is to work, you must harness the collective intelligence of the team.

To be effective, the leader must delegate responsibility and have a system that each person will report back to the manager or designated person in charge. If you don't do that, management will not know what's going on in the operation and cannot correct mistakes. No manager can personally manage everything alone.

Whenever I give my employee a task, I tell the person my expectations. I ask how soon he or she can deliver. If that person says two weeks, I note that in my calendar and follow up accordingly. Failure to establish upfront expectations can cause projects to flounder or fail.

A few years ago, Roberta and I gave some property to a university with the understanding that staffers would list the property for sale shortly thereafter. I noted this in my calendar, and late in that calendar year, I followed up to confirm the property had sold.

"What's the status?" I asked.

"We're going to get it listed," one executive said.

I took this matter directly to the president and advised him to set up a system of accountability. I knew that successful leadership is impossible if the task is not delegated with deadlines and expectations. If you don't manage employees like that, you don't know what your team is doing. The president agreed with me, but that didn't change the fact that more than half a year had been wasted.

I hold myself to the same standards as my employees. Whatever I'm doing, I estimate how much time it will take to complete the project. The act of writing down expectations and deadlines makes people more cognizant of their responsibilities.

When determining deadlines and expectations, it's best to involve the employee in the discussion. Ask the employee when he or she thinks the job will be completed, instead of dictating when it should be completed. That way, the employee owns the responsibility. The onus is on the employee. Once the employee gives me the date, I post it in my calendar and expect the job to be finished on time unless I agree to an extension.

It's Management 101, checks and balances. When I ask people to do something for me, the first thing I ask them is, "When?" If I'm going to be proficient as a manager, I have to know where every moving part is at all times. That's how I run things.

Later, if an employee comes to me and says, "You know, Dr. Jenkins, I said I was going to finish the job in a week, but because I had to take my wife to see her dying mother, it's going to take a little longer."

I give them the benefit of the doubt. I ask how much longer they think it will take. Then I rebook the task. Overall, I get my employees to buy into the game plan by handing them the time and objectives, which gives them a reason to stay engaged.

Just as in investing, I factor a margin of safety into all my management decisions. If I've got a bill that comes due on the fifteenth of the month, I schedule payment for the tenth. Managers who build a margin of safety into every decision get to enjoy the benefits of self-imposed checks and balances. My life is structured in the same way.

Many people say they can't live like that. They say they'd prefer to live footloose and fancy free. But if you want to accomplish things, you need structure and planning—a map and a moral compass of values to make sure you land at an honorable destination.

Planning makes life more interesting too because you've always got something positive on your mind. Throughout my life, I usually awake around three o'clock in the morning with a torrent of ideas rolling around in my head. I roll over, flip the light on, and start writing my daily to-do list, and when I get up, I start working on each item, checking them off as the day goes by. Each check is a positive step toward one of my game plans. Reaching goals that started as dreams is what makes my heart sing. Hard work, discipline, and sacrifice channeled into the implementation of a well-researched strategic game plan is an age-old formula for success in any endeavor.

Peter Drucker is considered a management visionary. His innovative approach to improving management techniques has impacted virtually every sector in the modern economy. But throughout his vast range of publications, one fundamental remains: the golden rule. Treat people the way you would like to be treated.

In an age when it was too often acceptable to denigrate employees, Drucker asserted that employees on every level of an organization should be treated with respect and valued for their job-related insights. I always enjoyed my talks with Drucker, and I'm proud that Roberta and I were honored with a plaque at the business school that bears his name. So much of good management amounts to simple, common decency.

Do you treat employees the way you treat your wife, son, or daughter? If not, you may want to reconsider your conduct. I treat every employee like family. If he or she is not performing according to standards, I review expectations with them and discuss ways to improve.

Keeping a positive work culture is important before, during, and after an employee's tenure. Never let an employee leave a job angry with you. You don't want them going out and spreading all kinds of toxic claims about you and your business.

In every phase of management, it is critical to create a culture of respect. Managers who interrupt their employees during meetings and generally project a lack of respect are shooting themselves in the foot. Managers who think they can treat employees poorly and then make up for it with Christmas bonuses are only fooling themselves. The best way to engender loyalty in an organization is to treat each person as a valuable team member.

You can't buy off your employees. They appreciate it if you pay them well, but you cannot skip respect and common decency. Your employees are invaluable repositories of operating knowledge. Listen to them because they are your eyes and ears in the field.

You can't be everywhere at all times. Your employees will make or break you. I always do exit interviews with my employees. During those interviews, I give them the opportunity to identify areas where the business could improve. I assure them that I will not become angry by anything they say.

Fellow business owners have questioned why I do this. How else can I access candid feedback from employees without that kind of departing interface? I may not agree with everything I hear during those interviews, but I always take note of the comments, addressing any matters that warrant further consideration for operational improvement.

Respect your employees, and they will respect you.

In 2008, we started selling off more of our real-estate holdings. Because of downsizing, we needed to let some people go. I met with my board and discussed how much severance pay we should give the departing employees. The board suggested three month's salary, but that didn't sit right with me. Some of those people had been with me for a long time. I decided to give them a year's pay. After some discussion, the board agreed. Now do you think those employees are going to go out and say bad things about us?

Of course not. We treated them like family. Sure, we could have legally given them much less in severance pay, but that would not have been right. By sharing the wealth, those good business values and resources transferred back to those outgoing employees' families and communities. I thought of it as uplifting America.

As a business owner, you want to cultivate a reputation in the community as somebody who other people want to work for and do business with. You want people saying, "Even if things don't *go* right, that business will *do* right by you."

Roberta and I are always touched when our employees tell us things like, "I've never worked for a company like yours, ever."

When our employees leave, for whatever reason, many leave crying and sad to go. Many of our past employees are still in touch with Roberta and me, many years after they leave.

There have been lots of books written about business ethics. Elected officials drone on and on about ethical practices. But at the end of the day, if you put your morals and values first, they will guide your business decisions, goals, and game plans.

If you let greed or fear or other negatives supersede your values, then those toxic desires will corrupt your priorities and decisions, and it's a slippery slope from there.

Business ethics are simple, but they are often presented in an extremely complicated manner. Implementing business ethics only gets complicated if your values are out of sync. It is a self-evident statement that business leaders who are always honest, always follow the law, and always uphold humanitarian values are far less likely to fall into corruption. But while this is generally true, it overlooks one important safeguard: avoiding conflicts of interest, even the appearance of a conflict.

Many well-intentioned people who aspire to ethical lives become ensnared in corruption because they have made previous decisions that set them up for trouble. That's why I was so adamant that members of the banking board never borrowed from our bank. Had I allowed members of the board to borrow from our bank rather than a larger corresponding bank that offered more extensive checks and balances, I would have increased the probability of corruption. Equally important, even if the board members ethically borrowed from our bank, it would send the wrong message to the public by creating the *appearance* of impropriety.

Avoiding even the appearance of all conflicts of interest is important in any social undertaking. Roberta and I always set up mentorship programs by pairing young women with older established women, and young men were placed with male mentors. Is this because we don't trust our mentors? No, it is simply because we wanted to reduce the possibility of the appearance of sexual misconduct. An ethical organization must visually and verbally represent its values if they are to take root in substance, policy, and appearance.

What I see in this country right now is a scourge of greed in the business world. If you go into business only to make money, that's a bad omen. Sadly, that is the explanation for why so many huge financial scandals have emerged over the last several years: people not taking responsibility for the consequences of their actions and dismissing their role in corrupt acts by saying, "Well, it was legal."

Such a pervasive mentality triggers a chain reaction: one company screws over another, one person screws over another, until people begin to accept that that's what business is all about.

In order to turn back the unethical tide in business, there needs to be more positive reinforcement, more people acting ethically and humanely, and in the process, representing to others that there are good people in our country who won't take advantage of you.

It's unfortunate that corrupt Wall Street firms have been permitted to quite explicitly hedge their bets against American main street businesses. Those who intentionally wasted people's personal retirements and college funds should be in jail. I cannot fathom betting against my own investors. My goal was always to get my investors' money working *for* them, not *against* them.

Everyone needs a broad view of our existence in this world to remind us of our inextricable link to humanity. By humanity, I'm speaking of human relationships—how you treat other human beings. That concern needs to be in the forefront of your dealings with people in business, in communities, and with family and friends.

Often people say, "Well, business is business." But I believe there should be a human face on business. At times, many people only show greed, destruction, and carelessness.

My biggest struggles in business have been racism in the financial sector and a lack of honesty. In the end, those struggles were driven by a lack of wholesome and humanitarian values, and it was those challenges that compelled me to transition into the third phase of my career—philanthropy.

I planned to use philanthropy and mentoring to promote positive values in businesses and communities around the country.

"How far you go in life depends on your being tender with the young, compassionate with the aged, sympathetic with the striving, and tolerant of the weak and strong. Because someday in your life, you will have been all of these" (George Washington Carver).

CHAPTER 25

Game Plan for Entrepreneurial Goals

Game plans are among the most ancient human mental processes. Every game plan, beginning with the first mammoth hunting expeditions to the development of computer-generated algorithms, is a strategy worked out in advance to reach a particular outcome.

When one of my game plans fails to secure my desired result, I concentrate on the positive things I can do to improve my results. The past is always behind me; I learn from it and never allow it to devastate me. This is an abiding mindset in my relentless pursuit of *positive possibilities*.

Many times, when I'm giving a lecture, the first thing I'll ask the audience is, "If I take my keys and give them to you and tell you to deliver my car to New York, what's the first thing you would do?"

Often, listeners in the audience will miss it, but some get it. "The first thing I'd do would be to pull out my road map," I say. "I'd go on Google, use the GPS, or crack open a road map, because then I'd know where I'm going. You need direction."

I've tried to plan everything important in my life—my marriage, my children, my business, as well as how to help others. And for all my planning and discipline, it never ceases to amaze me how surprising each day turns out, for better or for worse.

And there have been a lot of worse days.

Life is indeed a mystery and a crapshoot; game plans simply put you in the best position to assert your values and ambitions in the face of whatever comes your way. Usually, one has to fight more bad than good to enjoy life without fear, anxiety, or devastation.

Game plans enable you to define your own future. The point is to free yourself and to remove limitations and negativity before you define your goals and game plans.

If you're a young person just starting out, don't let your lack of experience make you timid. *Be bold!* Define goals that inspire you, and determine strategic game plans to attain those goals. If you're a seasoned veteran, don't let success make you complacent. And don't harbor negative feelings about past failures. Learn from both successes and failures, and apply that knowledge to establishing positive and strategic goals and game plans.

How does one set a bold yet achievable goal? Make sure your mind is clear and be prepared to focus one hundred percent on *positive possibilities*—a new mode of perception that compels you to look for the opportunity in every situation.

Now consider why goals matter. A goal is the stating of a desired result. I desire to compete in the Olympics. I desire to become a lawyer. I desire to retire when I'm forty-five. I desire to raise healthy, productive children. Desire is the first motivating factor to setting a goal, and without a game plan to see it through, it's useless.

What is a game plan? A game plan is a strategy to reach your goal. When crafting long-term goals, form a mind-set that eliminates all limitations. No matter what it looks like then, *nothing is impossible!* See it, believe it, feel it, do it.

I like to shock people. I like to take them to a mental environment they've never dared go before. When I walk out of a hotel and see a valet, a concierge, or a bellhop, no matter what ethnicity or what age, I'll ask, "Do you own this hotel?"

They're always shocked. "Me? No."

I press them. "You ever thought about it?"

"Can't say I have. No, I haven't."

"I bet if you thought about it, you could do it," I say, and then I move on.

I just gave them something to think about.

Your mind is working twenty-four hours a day, so you might as well put it to work for *you*. Use that mental activity to develop wise goals and innovative game plans, rather than wondering where the next party is or how to get even with someone for a real or imagined abuse.

For example, I trained my mind to become a captain in the air force instead of accepting a lower status. I figured out, planned, and implemented the strategic game plan of timing to meet my goal. If I hadn't used my thinking to figure out the steps for a better life, there's no way I could have gotten the education I needed for a better future.

If you start thinking like that, you can reach goals that previously seemed impossible. I encourage young children by asking them where they plan to attend college. Usually, they give me a quizzical look, but I keep pressing them.

"What do you want to do? What do you want to be?" Sometimes, they're shy and don't answer; or maybe just smile. But I imagine the gears turning in their impressionable brains.

Parents often approach me afterward and thank me for engaging with their children.

It has become second nature to me now. I've always believed I could do anything I wanted to do, so I give everyone else the same respect. I recall Ron Burkle from when I served on the Claremont Graduate University Board of Directors with him. He started his career as a bag boy at a Stater Brothers grocery store. He worked himself up the ranks, and now he's a billionaire with holdings in grocery stores and many other businesses. The point is this: if you think constructive thoughts, you will do constructive things. If you think destructive thoughts, you're more likely to do destructive things.

You are what you think.

There are billions of cells in our brains, and in a lifetime, we only use several hundred million of them. Always think *positive possibilities*—every minute, every hour, every day. They are right there in front of you, almost invisible. Look closer!

It was Charles Fourier, the French philosopher, who declared that "the future of man would grow out of the brain of man, shaped, controlled, and directed by his desires and passions." There are comparatively few people with great desires. Many are content to accept the mediocrity allowed to fall on them. Some blame their lack of success upon everyone but their own thinking. The goal seeker never realizes that it's just as easy to shoot a bird on a high limb as it is to shoot one on the ground. Desire is the driving force. So learn to create great desires.

But how do we create that desire?

We create desire by recognizing that human beings can transform the mediocre into the extraordinary. Excellence displays the difference between the average sports player and the superstar, between success and failure.

Take Jason Williams, otherwise known as White Chocolate, known for loving basketball. He was only six feet tall and therefore had to play guard. So he studied his competition and developed a game plan to become a tremendous dribbler and passer. Because his father worked at a school, Williams would go there and practice dribbling and passing in the gymnasium until 2:00 a.m. He was a white guy who learned to handle the ball like many of the best black superstars. That's how he got the nickname White Chocolate.

Williams worked hard and pushed himself to meet the competition he would encounter in the NBA. He was named to the NBA's All-Rookie Team in 1999 and won a championship with the Miami Heat in 2006.

When I was young, my mother often said, "Take what you've got and make what you want." At the same time, she helped me cultivate the ability to see the hidden possibilities all around me. *Positive possibilities* is the art of seeing resources others do not and applying them to your desired result.

Education is the great equalizer when it comes to identifying *positive possibilities*. The more you know, the more opportunities you can identify. As a lifelong student of the world, I seek to know about as many things as possible.

In the early '80s, I gave a speech to high school students, encouraging them to keep updating their skills and knowledge. I told them the world would be far more technologically oriented in the future.

We were in the information age that was morphing into the technology age, and everything was changing at a rapid speed.

To cope with those changes, I believed it was essential that students go to college or trade school. Graduates from such schools and programs would, on average, earn more than twice as much as their counterparts with only a high school diploma. Even after finishing high school and earning a degree, graduates need to continually take refresher courses to keep up with changing technology.

To give broad context to my thesis about technology, I told the students that "Nations, including the United States, have spent billions of dollars on huge seagoing vessels. But the missiles used in the Falklands War signaled that those ships would soon be obsolete."

I explained that missiles could travel twenty miles straight, eluding interceptors by traveling only ten feet above the water, in order to hit their targets. The Falklands War demonstrated that future wars would increasingly be fought by computers. The centrality of computers would also hold true in the public and private sectors. Wars are now fought using unmanned drones that are remotely operated at computer terminals thousands of miles away.

As an example of spotting *positive possibilities*, I quickly identified the potential for pet insurance. The same held true for manufactured housing, where most of my wealth originated. I also identified the method of military warfare—that computers, and later the Internet, would bring about.

Does that make me clairvoyant? Am I some kind of genius? No. It means I remained engaged, well-read, and driven. I remained a student of innovation and trends.

Those habits have kept me tapped into my biggest resources for years. As a result, I can have in-depth discussions on many topics: international affairs, scientific and economic news, war and peace. The ability to have those discussions opens many doors in a social and economic context. A life of engaged reading and active listening has allowed me to contribute knowledge to posterity and further, just a bit, the reach of the human mind.

Even today, I don't feel adequate if I don't have reading materials available to me. I want to know about the Federal Reserve Board, international news, and scientific and technological breakthroughs, although it never hurts to read the sports page first!

Many people are at a staggering disadvantage by their choice not to read; they are placed at a competitive disadvantage when it comes to seeing *positive possibilities*. When it comes time for parents to nurture their children with an insatiable curiosity about life, they fall short. It troubles me that the old tradition of taking children to the library seems to be dying fast.

One of the best things a parent can do for his or her children is read to them. Then after reading to their children, they should read themselves rather than turning on the TV. Parents will always need new information to challenge their children.

Remember, children don't always listen to what you say, but they always watch what you do.

Several years ago, we were traveling in Spain, and I left the hotel to get some reading material. When I returned, my son Dexter was in our suite.

"Where were you?" I asked.

"I went down to get a newspaper," he said.

That brightened my day, knowing I had given to my son one of the most valuable things I could give him besides unconditional love: curiosity about the world around him. I had passed the baton to the next generation.

Two other essential qualities I suggest that parents pass to their children are resilience and diligence. I learned that as a child on the family farm, working from dusk till dawn, but always loving the satisfaction of a job well done and the camaraderie of my siblings.

Today, especially in the cities and suburbs, it seems like too many kids grow into adults who are couch potatoes. They're tired even before they start the day. Children are born with boundless energy and curiosity. If they're taught to harness that vital life force in constructive ways, they will benefit from it for the rest of their lives. Children who are given a good foundation of wholesome, humanitarian values will generate a confident outlook and be less likely to get into trouble.

I've always been happy in my life. I've never had a point when I've been depressed. Sure, I've been disappointed, but disappointment is temporary. I've been knocked down plenty, but I always got back up.

The human mind is astonishingly powerful. Some years back, there was a young runner, Guy Grutsch, who felt a sharp pain in his right thigh when he was about one-third into his race. He continued and finished with an impressive time. After crossing the finish line, his muscles relaxed and lost support of the bone. He collapsed. When he was rushed to the hospital, x-rays showed that he had suffered a fracture in his femur and would have ordinarily not been able to move. That runner had crossed the line on sheer desire. So if you desire something desperately in life, you have to aim for the goal with great passion, no matter the consequences.

After a half century of almost no official communication with Cuba, President Barack Obama opened relations with that island nation during the last year of his presidency.

With permission from both the Obama administration and the Cuban government, the Long Beach Latin American Museum of Art sponsored a cultural exchange visit, and Roberta and I were able to join the group.

We flew directly from LAX to Havana. They offered each of us rum as a gesture of friendship. The only bad part about it was that the stuff tasted so good I asked for another swig and it nearly took off the top of my head!

We were very impressed with the beauty of the buildings. They had a regal bearing that was not diminished by many years of deferred maintenance, which told the tale of decisions made by the hard-boiled leadership. The United States embargo that prevented them from purchasing new cars had been in place for five decades, and the people were driving vintage '55, '56, and '57 Fords and Chevy's almost exclusively. It was almost like entering a time machine. The beaches were gorgeous. The water was a magnificent deep blue with large swaths of glistening white sand under bright, sparkling sunshine.

One day, while observing the scenery and reading a book, a young Cuban stood nearby eyeing my sneakers. Finally, he said, "Sir, will you give me your shoes?" After the shock of his request, I took the young man to a local store and bought him a pair of sneakers just like mine. After he left, I went back to reading my book. When I glanced up, there he stood again running toward me with all his buddies behind him. It was time to move into the marketplace and hear the local talk and feel the culture.

European and Canadian men had descended on Havana, as they did every year for weeks, to take up with Cuban women as though they were married. The people talked openly about it.

The most adverse aspect of Cuban society was the shortage of simple things like paper and pencils. It was economic slavery. Some of that seemed to be changing since the embargo was slowly being lifted, giving the people a little more freedom, hope, and opportunity. Many Cubans escaped the hard conditions, but many died. The ones that survived proved that anything is possible. I believe that with every fiber of my being. I have lived my entire life by that principle.

Yes, anything is possible!

CHAPTER 26

⋘❈⋙

Socializing for Business
and Pleasure

It was Christmas 2010 in California when Roberta and I decided to attend a holiday party in downtown Long Beach. When we arrived at the high-rise office building, we joined the festivities, catching up with old friends and meeting new acquaintances. Eventually, I took a seat, leaned back, and just observed the party, a business affair with a range of successful professionals and community leaders.

Shortly thereafter, a white gentleman in his fifties or sixties sat next to me, and we began to talk. We discussed work, business, and current events. The conversation rambled on predictably and amiably until we began talking about our children.

"Kids are different today," I said. "This whole generation is different."

He nodded and told me he had two grown daughters who were both married.

"Are you happy with their mates?" I asked.

He paused a moment. "Well, I don't know. I'm conflicted."

"What do you mean?"

He hesitated again before continuing. Obviously, my question was unexpected, and the answer was of great concern. "I taught my kids to be tolerant, but I never thought things would turn out like they did."

"How did things turn out?"

"Well, one of them married a Vietnamese man, and the other married a black guy."

Many people would have taken offense at his statement, but something in this man's naked honesty told me to be gentle. "Well, you shouldn't feel too bad about that," I said. "After all, everybody came from Africa."

He just looked at me.

"Did you know that?" I asked.

"No, I didn't."

I told him he might want to watch a recent PBS documentary called *The Journey of Man* even though I knew it would take more than a movie recommendation to address this man's confusion and angst about race.

The holiday party chatter muted, the music faded, and the immediate scene became the story I was about to tell. Our minds were in Africa. "The first known human beings are from Africa," I began. "We all came from Africa—everyone."

I looked into the man's eyes and saw a puzzled stranger's eyes, or perhaps, they were inwardly scolding. I wondered what his look meant, but I pressed on.

"Originally, all humans were dark-skinned because the powerful African sun stimulated the production of melanin, which is the skin's natural protective pigment. Similarly, the original Africans had dark curly hair to protect their skulls from the hot sun. They had wide noses with broad nostrils so that air could be easily carried to the brain to cool it in hot weather."

I knew what I was saying could seem odd to the uninitiated, so I told the story of the great human migration out of Africa with great care, periodically stopping to gauge my fellow partygoer's responses. His eyes signaled a keen interest, so I continued.

"Humans are like animals in this respect—they evolved in response to environmental changes. Take the polar bear. It was originally a brown bear, but over the millennia, it migrated to cold climates and no longer needed dark fur to protect its skin. So its fur turned white, which enabled it to camouflage itself with snow, making it a more proficient arctic hunter."

There's beauty and art in good conversation. Like captivating books, they teach new things and fresh concepts of reality. I sensed that maybe I had found a *positive possibility* to ease a non-needed pain in this miserable man's mind. My new acquaintance remained engaged, and I proceeded with my brief history of the first and only race on earth: the human race.

"The first known migration out of Africa was to Australia. It took those first people a thousand years to get there. Some of the original root people are now the Aborigines. Meanwhile, people kept migrating out of Africa. And what a migration it was. Those early humans were pursuing better lives, riding the crest of human curiosity and ingenuity to new horizons. Through valleys, across plains and rivers—weathering storms, hunting and fending off wild animals, raising children, and tending to the elderly and the sick. They survived because they cared about each other. They survived because they cooperated as a race in the natural competition for life-sustaining resources.

"The human beings who went into the coldest climates, like the brown bears that evolved into polar bears, turned lighter in complexion. There was no need to protect the skull from the sun because the sun didn't shine as much, and over a period of time, their hair grew stringier, as is usually the case with people from cold climates. In colder climates, the noses typically narrow because it's no longer advantageous to carry as much air to the brain. On the contrary, staying warm requires keeping the cold air out.

"So much of the history of the human race is just practical common sense. Take vitamin D. Without it, humans cease to metabolize calcium properly, their bones and muscles grow weak, and chances of cardiovascular diseases and cancer increase. Making this long story shorter, humans cannot survive without sufficient vitamin D.

"Fortunately, the human body produces vitamin D in response to sunlight. In Africa and other warm environments, vitamin D is easily accessed. But in cold climates, where people were bundled up, often uncovering little more than their faces, it's more difficult to access vitamin D.

"So early humans in cold climates developed lighter complexions with less melanin, and they were able to absorb as much sunlight as possible. The only dark-skinned populations in cold climates were people who lived in coastal regions where seafood rich in vitamin D was plentiful.

"Because humans have lived for such a short period of time, it has been historically difficult for people to understand how slow and subtle evolutionary changes take place. They change over countless generations and have made each of us the people we are. The great gift of living in the twenty-first century is that, with each passing year, new scientific histories are written with evidence derived from DNA, which is shedding light on human genetic history.

"Through the collaborative efforts of evolutionary geneticists, geographic information systems specialists, anthropologists, archeologists, historians, linguists, and others, a new understanding of the origins of the human race now exists. Through digitally analyzing DNA extracted from human blood samples taken from all corners of the world, it is clear that every fourth living human is related and all human migrations trace back to African origin. Human history is written in our blood, so says the geneticist Spencer Wells, the author of *The Journey of Man*, which inspired the PBS documentary I told you about.

"He points out that within each DNA sample exists thousands of years of evolutionary history. By correlating differences in DNA with the histories of human migrations, researchers can map human journeys out of Africa and into Southern Asia and beyond."

That was probably the longest speech I'd ever given to just one person in a very long time, but he clearly needed an education, and I saw the opportunity and ran with it.

That white man sitting next to me was either completely awed or totally disturbed by my speech because he was struck dumb for a solid couple of minutes.

Finally, he muttered, "I've never heard of anything like that."

I smiled. "Check out that documentary," I said and rose to find Roberta.

He stood up as well. "We all came from the same tribe," I said.

"What was that show called again?"

"*Journey of Man*," I said, taking his question as a *positive possibility*.

We parted as friends, I think, and I hope he watched that program.

Maybe the history I shared with that man, if shared more widely, could keep parents of any race from teaching hatred to their children. Because hatred is *learned*, which means it's *taught*, by parents to their children, mostly.

When he first sat down next to me, that well-intentioned but ill-informed gentleman viewed himself as distinctly different from me. But after our conversation, he hopefully realized that he and I, like his Vietnamese son-in-law and his black son-in-law, really were all part of the same tribe—the human race.

Thinking along those lines, it seems to me that there is more than one kind of evolution. Society, like human beings, *evolves*, hopefully in a good way, but not always. Sometimes, it takes a while to right itself. As Dr. Martin Luther King, Jr. once said, "The arc of the moral universe is long, but it bends towards justice."

Before the 1954 Brown versus Board of Education decision that outlawed school segregation, black schools routinely included black history in their curricular; whereas, once schools were integrated, if black history were taught at all, it was so benign and varnished over that one might not consider it to be of any impact at all in American history. Ignoring the race issue in America resulted in whole groups of Americans being uninformed on the traumatizing impact on all of its citizens.

Now in California and other states, educators, school boards, and politicians are being pushed for policies and laws that include multiethnic history in classrooms, rather than excessive Eurocentric studies. This is being done to accommodate the rapidly changing demographics.

For as long as I've spoken in public, I've recommended a book that uncovers the unvarnished truth about slavery, Jim Crow, and discrimination in America. Supporters of those discriminatory acts had designs of colonizing it not only across the Southern United States but also throughout Latin America and South America. The name of the book is *A Peoples History of the United States* by Howard Zinn. It is called by some, *The Bible on Race in America*.

We are now living in a very diverse culture, where no one knows what in-laws, grandchildren, mates, or others might look like. I believe that Howard Zinn's book will be a great aid in calming the troubled waters of racial anxiety and uncertainty.

It may take us a while to get there, but that arc always points in the right direction.

CHAPTER 27

Bright Future

It wasn't the white man's ideology that rendered me mute for most of the ride home from the party, but it did take me back to the reality of a bad memory. In fact, it recovered three tragic events in my life where racism cut me to the core.

The first and most hurtful racist act included my only daughter, Sabrae. It happened when she was a teenager, but the wound was so deep that it gripped me and rendered me mute for a time. Sabrae was crying and crying, and it was something I couldn't fix, at least not right then. Maybe I couldn't fix it at all.

When Sabrae was thirteen, she had mostly white girlfriends, as she attended a predominately white school. Her friends would come over and swim in our pool. They'd sleep over in our home, and she'd sleep over in theirs. It didn't seem to matter that she was black and they were white; they were just friends having fun, all growing from the same ancient tribe. But when those girls reached thirteen, it seemed that a need to maintain the generational separatism cut her out.

For several weekends, her friends would come back to school whispering about places they had gone, friends they had seen, and fun that they'd had. When she asked them about it, they explained that she wouldn't want to go because their other friends might not like her.

That rejection cut Sabrae to the core. How does a close friend slip away and leave and tell you it's not for you to know about because their other white friends might not like you and they don't want you to be hurt?

Sabrae couldn't stop crying. When Roberta told me what was going on, I dropped everything and held my daughter close, whispering over and over, "It's going to be all right."

I loved my daughter without end, and to see her crying and hurting like that was like enduring surgery without anesthesia. Her brokenness matched my helplessness at that moment. She loved her friends, and I loved her, but I had no means of repairing her wound. I didn't know whether it could *be* repaired. I wanted to reach into her beautiful soul and rip that pain away, but I couldn't.

The worst feeling in the world for a parent is a child who's hurting.

Finally, she looked up in my face, her eyes swollen and red. "Daddy, I hate white people."

Though stunned, I felt the root of her outburst, and I pulled her close. I took a deep breath and began to talk to her pain. I believed the right questions could heal my child.

It was my duty and responsibility to teach a lesson in humanity to my daughter at one of the most painful moments of her young life. Roberta and I had raised Sabrae around people of many cultures and ethnicities. Our family regularly vacationed with Chinese, Jewish, and white families. We had explored the world together with those families. Those trips created fond memories for our entire family, including Sabrae.

I wiped the tears from her face. "Do you hate Dr. Fink and Dr. Bergquist and their kids?"

"No," Sabrae answered.

"How about Yvonne—you hate her?"

Sabrae shook her head no. Her red nose and swollen eyes seemed to pulse with hurt and anger.

"What about Jan—you hate her?"

"No," she said.

"So it's not really about white people, is it?"

She shrugged.

In time, Sabrae got over that painful episode, but she never forgot how badly it felt. People don't realize how much they hurt others when they discriminate against them. And in many cases, they don't even realize they're doing it. They are careless about other people's lives, without a thought.

I'm so thankful that neither I nor any of my family members were ever taught to discriminate. We always had people from all walks of life as family, friends, coworkers, social partners, classmates, and colleagues. I had experienced plenty of discrimination before that day, but I'll never forget how that one incident broke something in me. It stirred some resolve deep inside as I held my sobbing daughter in my arms.

The sound of her little heart against my chest just about broke my own in two. She was so innocent and vulnerable. I reminded her of the wisdom of the golden rule—do unto others as you would have them do unto you.

To get an idea of the importance of the role that parents play in shaping their children's views on race, consider a recent study conducted by child psychologist Dr. Melanie Killen. The study examines how and why children attribute positive, neutral, or negative attitudes to people from different racial backgrounds. Those attitudes, of course, determine how children treat others and who they embrace as friends.

In other words, children are what they are taught to be.

The remainder of this text is singularly dedicated to presenting a new vision for our nation and our planet earth. That vision sees a future full of *positive possibilities*. A bright future will require people to open their eyes to "invisible injustice to visible justice."

As I drove home after that party, I recalled an old book I read many years ago in college: *The Invisible Man* by Ralph Ellison.

I always tried to go in everyone's way but my own. I have also been called one thing and then another, while no one really wished to hear what I called myself. So after years of trying to adopt the opinions of others, I finally rebelled. I am an invisible man.

In Ellison's classic novel, first published in 1952, the black man who is the narrator remains anonymous. He sees a country full of people who are blinded, willfully or involuntarily, by their attitudes toward him as a black man. As a result, he has gone underground to examine his life while he relates it to us, the reader. Today, sixty-one years after *The Invisible Man* was published, I find that my black skin still makes me invisible to many people.

Here was the awakening of the invisible man, another hurtful experience.

Not too long ago, I attended the California State University Foundation Board of Directors dinner. I sat at a table with ten members and the chancellor of the board. The chancellor, sitting next to me, introduced every board member around the table to people who came over to pay their respects, all except me.

After realizing that I was not going to be introduced, I stood, held out my hand, and introduced myself. As soon as the greeters left, I turned to the chancellor and looked him straight in the eye.

"I'm a board member," I said. "Why didn't you introduce me to the people who stopped by?"

"I, I," he hesitated, unable to form an explanation.

I allowed him to stutter without interruption. Finally, he could only shrug. "I didn't realize I hadn't introduced you," he said. "I feel terrible about it."

I believed that he didn't realize he hadn't introduced me, and I also believed that he felt badly about it. But I understood quite well why he didn't introduce me. Black life in the presence of many whites did not matter. To that man, at that time, I was invisible.

George Franklin Grant was a pioneering dentist, the first African American professor at Harvard, and an inventor. He was most often recognized in his day for inventing a prosthetic for nonsurgical rehabilitation of people with cleft palates. But he was never acknowledged in a way that did justice to that accomplishment. Today, he is widely remembered as an avid golfer who invented the first wooden golf tee, which he patented in 1899.

As one of the first minority persons to play golf in the United States, Grant was no stranger to discrimination. As a young man caddying for a white woman, he noticed that every time they walked the fairway, she passed intestinal gas, but when she was around her playing partners, she did not. In other words, Grant surmised that this woman considered him to be invisible.

Golf, like so many other American pastimes, has been marred by its social separation by race. The Augusta National didn't admit a black member until 1990. Seven years later, Tiger Woods became the first nonwhite person and youngest player ever to win at Augusta. Woods's victory coincided with the fiftieth anniversary of Jackie Robinson breaking the baseball color barrier.

In the foreword to *Uneven Lies*, Woods recalls his first experience at Augusta in 1995. "The first time I drove down Magnolia Lane, I was not thinking about Bobby Jones or what all the Masters stood for," he writes. "I was thinking about all the great African American players who never got a chance to play there."

Woods's reflection pays homage to Lee Elder, who in the face of death threats became the first African American to compete at Augusta in 1975. During that time, Elder had to change clothes in his car because he was not allowed in the clubhouse.

Lee Trevino, who celebrated his Mexican heritage on and off the course, frequently commented on the racist climate at Augusta. The first female members were not admitted to Augusta until 2012. Thankfully, Augusta's national culture of racism and sexism are gradually changing. But the country club's stubborn resistance to including anyone other than rich white men is a perfect example of what happens when individuals, groups, or institutions embrace racist, elitist, or sexist views that regard one group of people as inferior to another.

The thought of it stirred another old memory.

Roberta's sister, Patricia Jones, was the first student to integrate a public school in her hometown of Bath, South Carolina. Although she was an *A* student and always raised her hand to answer the teacher's questions, the only time the white teacher called on her was when no one else knew the answer. Apparently, she was invisible.

I would have fixed all that for my precious daughter with love, compassion, and integrity, but I just didn't have enough left in me to extinguish the ingrained hatred that caused her pain in the first place. There was so much resistance to humility that it never seemed to be reached.

Now as I drove home, listening to the sounds of the cool winter night, the impartial roar of the ocean waves, a distant honking of a car horn, I thought of how well *positive possibilities* had served my daughter and me when I taught her that love always triumphs over hate.

"It's how we survive, Sabrae."

And she did.

As I pulled my car into the garage, I pushed the memory of her pain back into the dark recesses of my mind and instead marveled at the amazing woman she had since become.

It's how we survive.

CHAPTER 28

❖❖❖

Tuskegee Looms Larger than the Past or the Present

Mr. Lonnie Hooks, permanent driver for Tuskegee's president, picked me up at the Atlanta airport. Along the way to the school, I kept reflecting on experiences as a student there. The warm feelings reminded me of those times. The moment I spotted Old Montgomery Road, I recalled when Roberta and I first walked to the movies together, laughing and talking all the way.

That thought was only interrupted by seeing Phelps Hall, where the veterinary students lived. Girls from the dorm next door would often throw rocks up to my second-floor window to get attention. Sometimes, they would yell invitations for me to join them for some event. I just never had the time to go.

By the time we cruised past the cafeteria, I recalled lovely Roberta Jones descending those stairs that Saturday afternoon. Prior to that time in my life, I couldn't trust myself with any emotional attachments that would possibly conflict with my studies. So I had never pursued her.

In my senior year, that long walk down Old Montgomery Road going to the movies with Roberta captured my heart.

My driver turned onto the campus streets, leading to the part of the veterinary school where I used to walk with Dr. Patterson, former Tuskegee president and founder of UNCF. I still remember what he said to me on one of our morning walks: "Young man, you're going to be very wealthy one day. When you are, I want you to give to others and offer a helping hand."

The vet school came into full view, and then all those 3:00 a.m. memories returned. I would be the only person working in the lab, cleaning petri dishes and test tubes while music from my little eight-dollar radio broke the silence.

Finally, the driver drove toward the Kellogg Center, the university's hotel, where Roberta and I would soon spend the entire year in the master suite because Grey Columns, the president's home, was in need of major remodeling. I felt proud that the Matthew and Roberta Jenkins Family Foundation had funded the recent remodeling of the hotel's lobby, bar, and restaurant.

For this project, we hired Vickie Carter (Tuskegee Graduate School of Architecture). She would also oversee the remodeling project and decorate the president's home.

Across the street from the hotel stood the Booker T. Washington Monument, which showed the university's founder lifting the veil of ignorance from his people. A stretch of green grass dotted with old southern brick and modern buildings showed off Tuskegee's proud heritage and my past and, hopefully, my future. I couldn't wait to get started with the restoration of Mother Tuskegee, bringing her back to the peak of her educational and financial powers through academic and vocational excellence.

Roberta joined me a few weeks later, and we toured the campus. Frankly speaking, I was almost speechless. My heart dropped when I saw how standards had dropped so far below my expectations.

Young men along our path wore pants halfway down their backsides. Both young men and young women walked past with their shoelaces untied and dragging. It looked like they'd trip and fall at any minute. Most of them failed to greet us even when we spoke to them first. The atmosphere represented anything but the social and academic environment one would expect at Tuskegee University. Those things matter.

When Roberta and I went to our quarters, we discussed a plan to turn things around. We decided to focus on engaging students to make the changes, rather than disrespecting the potential of their minds. It was important to us not to turn them off. I realized that some of the students would graduate at the end of my school year and would have to compete in finding their places in the corporate marketplace.

We wanted Tuskegee students to be presentable, respectful, amenable, warm, and approachable (PRAWA). They had a long way to go and a short time to get there. We had been entrusted with helping to improve their employment prospects, and I didn't plan to lose.

On that cool fall morning, we walked into the student body organization (SBO) and found our way into a meeting with one of the members. I used my tactic of asking questions.

"What do you think about the campus today? Do you feel confident that you will get a job that pays you a sufficient amount to take care of a family? How confident are you that you will get a job at all? Who do you think your competition is for that job? What do you think we can do together to make a difference? Can we make a difference?" I ran through all those questions and broke them down.

Roberta and I spent almost two hours discussing the pros and cons of those questions. In fact, the member brought in two others to deepen and solidify some of the concerns and think of ways to answer those concerns. After two hamburgers and lemonade, we had come up with one answer: we have to get the students on board, all them, to some degree. There were answers, and we had to find them.

At the meeting that followed, the president of the student government association and I set up a two-prong public relations blitz for campus students and the off-campus community. We hammered out the details, and finally, we had the topic and plan for the first collaborative effort between the university community and me, as interim president. We put our public relations juices to work through the students.

On the day of our meeting, we met in the university chapel, and the place was packed. Townspeople, community leaders, faculty, and staff showed up. Murmurs went through the crowd. Attendance was impressive.

I walked onto the stage and greeted the audience. "Students, staff, and members of the community. I called this meeting to get to know you better. I want you to know I'm on your side. But I also need your help. We need to work together to get a much-needed job done before your graduation this coming spring. Today, I want to talk about the ingredients of success."

I recalled my mother using the same words that were forming in my mouth.

"If we all put our shoulders to the wheel and push at the same time, we can do this."

I turned to the right side of the audience.

"I'm disturbed with what I see on campus. I see low hanging pants and long dragging shoelaces. I see a lack of communication between visitors and students. I see things that can keep you from getting a good job after you leave here, and I want to help. This is an incredible university with some of the most celebrated alumni in the Black University Network. We can do better.

"We all need to treat others as we want to be treated. How would you like to smile and speak to someone and watch as he or she looked the other way and ignored you?"

"The human resource person of almost any good company is trained to spot a badly trained demeanor in a single glance. They look at your appearance, attitude, and approachability. Will they hire you or someone else? That person judges your image and character before you even say a word to them. Like it or not, that's the way things are, and we can do better.

"What kind of inner character are you developing? Do you answer with monosyllables or complete sentences? Do you display your good character? Sometimes, it's as simple as a smile.

"You need to look healthy and be healthy. You need to take good care of yourselves. Imagine how an employer feels if you're sick every other week.

"We want to see you with jobs worthy of more than minimum wage. We want to see you going to graduate schools, getting vocational certifications. We want to see you grow, to succeed in life. There's a lot of competition out there, and we want you to be ready."

After an hour of sharing my thoughts, I was exhausted. But I was still willing to fight for them too.

"We want to give you the power to do something great with your lives, to accomplish whatever you want, to realize your dreams. Are you with me?"

I was gratified with a roar of agreement and a standing ovation. It felt good. When they settled down, I started up again.

"Everyone has a purpose. Serving your purpose in life makes the world a better place. What is your purpose?"

The crowd cheered again. I really thought I had gotten through to them.

Yet in the following days, we had serious pushback. Some staff members told the students that I was talking down to them; nevertheless, I met with the student government association, and we discussed the students' problems and concerns, trying to assess how many we had gotten on board.

A few days after the meeting, one of the SGA members, Asya Steele, came to my office and asked for help in promoting a seminar for the young women. The prior year, the organization had failed to get support from the administration. She and her committee presented their plan for a women's empowerment workshop: "High Heels in High Places."

I immediately asked her to call Roberta for help and expertise.

The following day, the two women met, and in one afternoon, they created a plan of extraordinary motivation and participation. Within weeks, it attracted powerful alumni, speakers, and supporters from across the region to share their expertise and resources with the students. The event was a huge success with both students and staff.

We moved ahead by planning a similar program for the male students. The president of SGA, Kyle Spencer, and his committee hosted an event called, "Men of Distinction."

The leaders stressed the importance of action, attitude, appearance, time management, and hard work. Their assignment was to follow the plan we had laid out for success.

The Matthew and Roberta Jenkins Family Foundation helped sponsor the luncheons, and those two seminars were suggested as annual events. Students became involved. Soon, I had great response from most departments at Tuskegee, and eventually, the pushback died down.

—◈◈◈—

 I called the faculty together and encouraged them to establish the International Student Exchange Program to offer students exposure to different cultures, as a means of personal growth.

My wife and I had traveled to many countries across the world, and we wanted that exposure for our students. From another nation's culture, you gain insight into why people desire to visit the United States. If our students could visit foreign countries, they would acquire a better understanding of their good fortune and make better use of the incredible benefits and resources they had in America.

I am honored to say that when my interim presidency came to an end, the students were moving toward upward mobility.

CHAPTER 29

⋆⟨⟨⟩⟩⋆

Tough Decisions, Favorable Returns

By the end of my year as interim president, we had begun to rehabilitate closed buildings and set a reserve for maintenance. We remodeled much-needed dorms to kick-start new student enrollment, beginning in the fall of 2014.

It seems that Tuskegee no longer represented the historical leadership of Booker T. Washington, George Washington Carver, Fredrick Patterson, and Luther Foster. During that period, it had a very strong and involved board of trustees. In my opinion, the lack of a strong board of overseers was the most prominent reason the university's standards seemed to drift away from its historical high expectations.

Tuskegee executives didn't seem to care about negotiating for better prices and services. When I became aware of such business practices, we renegotiated several contracts and saved almost $1.5 million in the process. We reduced the number of automobiles needed, phones, laptops, and other large ticket items.

My administration would no longer accept the "no accountability" mind-set with which staff and others had become comfortable. We set up checks and balances, time management, functional accountability, and efficiency. We made a habit to under-promise and over-deliver. We created and used the "five-minute plan," which meant getting to meetings five minutes before start time. All contracts and purchases had to be approved by department heads. Deferred maintenance for all buildings had to be discussed and acted upon annually.

Rumors went out that I was firing people. I answered, "I don't fire people, they fire themselves. If they did a good job, they're still here. If they didn't, they fired themselves."

My team and I finally concluded that the school of engineering was the department where countless opportunities could move Tuskegee forward, boost enrollment, and expand the school. There were many reasons we promoted our school of engineering. Large companies and the federal government were short of engineers. They needed to meet quotas in terms of demographics and diversity. Tuskegee could help alleviate that need.

I mentioned that we needed to double or triple the number of engineering students, as I thought the goal was easily attainable. It was based upon feedback from Boeing and the Department of Defense. "We like your engineers. We want more of them," they said.

When we talked to leadership in the school of engineering, they failed to see the *positive possibilities* there, but I kept the broad vision for that department to grow the student body and improve the university's culture.

During my year at Tuskegee, the search for a new president was ongoing. And as I had served on quite a few presidential search committees over the years, people would often ask what requirements were most needed in the potential president. I was always consistent with the goals of ongoing growth, quality education, and fiscal responsibility.

After forty odd years of assisting with the selection of various university presidents, I still support the four qualities and characteristics of a good president:

1) Good personnel skills, knowing how to deal with people fairly, firmly, honestly.
2) Integrity.

3) Good business skills—they are indispensable because they have a lot to do with the art of negotiating and being persuasive.

4) Management skills. Enforcing checks and balances are necessary for a smooth and accountable operation.

After one of the previous presidents of Tuskegee University had been selected, he went to meet the veterinary alumni. After his introduction, the body began to discuss allocating funds and how those funds should be managed. The new president stood up and straightened his shoulders.

"I'm the new president, and I will tell you up front—from here on, if you send money into Tuskegee, we do what we want with it. If you don't like it, you can keep your damned money."

Even a child would have known he had no people skills. So I knew something had to be done in the executive segment of the university to make Tuskegee whole again, and it needed to be done fast.

After several meetings and discussions, I laid out my game plan to make Tuskegee an outstanding university again. First of all, it had to recover a healthy culture and a financially sound bottom line. Whatever it took, I was willing to do it.

CHAPTER 30

Polished Game Plan

As the end of my tenure as interim president of Tuskegee drew near, I took a look at the administration for the previous thirty years. There seemed to have been a lack of passion for the school's productivity and for the education that would enable the students to grow with the nation. Every decline added up to that conclusion.

When I served on the Tuskegee Board of Trustees in the early '80s, I decided to quit primarily because I felt it was not carrying out the dictates of what our university's education should be—a vibrant atmosphere with the free exchange of ideas supported by passion and care for the fabric of the university. Instead, it grew to be dictatorial in nature. It was a climate that neither student nor leadership could fake. The test had been taken, the grades were in, and the result was staring us all in the face.

I set out to emphasize the concept of best business and person-nel practices to faculty, staff, and students, at every level of participa-tion in the Tuskegee community.

Here is what I set as my policies: give people good customer service, because when you do, they will become ambassadors and spokespersons for the university.

Treating people right pays dividends.

We made people feel welcome again by engaging them and finding out what their needs were. When we found what the needs were, we serviced them. Even the president was expected to follow those policies. We knew that if everyone worked in unison, the results would anchor the growth and stability of the university.

Having been at Tuskegee for almost a year, I planned to give a state of the university speech, entitled, "Changing Our Culture." The title didn't refer solely to Tuskegee University but to the African American culture as well.

I like to address issues in a broad context because what happened at Tuskegee was a microcosm of what was happening all over the United States. I talked to faculty about research and about increasing research potential for professors. In particular, I mentioned instituting a policy of incentives as a means of encouraging their research potential. I stressed the need for efficient time management, starting all meetings on schedule, as well as the importance of checks and balances.

The changes were aimed at changing the culture at Tuskegee. I was determined to turn things around. I made sure that if a meeting were to start at ten o'clock, then it started at ten o'clock sharp.

If attendees know you'll start on time, they will be there on time. If they know you start late, they will be late. Time management is one of the key educational elements I wanted to implant into the culture of Tuskegee before leaving.

In my opinion, there were three main factors stagnating enrollment at Tuskegee University:

1) Student Housing: routinely placing reserves in the budget for deferred maintenance would take care of that issue. Already we were seeing positive results in new students arriving.

2) Good Customer Service: I can't stress enough how important this person-to-person relationship was to the success of the university. When you create an atmosphere of friendliness and helpfulness, the public will become your ambassadors.

3) Health Services: parents were becoming quite concerned about the availability of health care services. We worked with the city of Tuskegee and identified a health care provider who wanted to provide plans to extend our health care emergency capability. Other noticeable health-related problems among the students were a high

incidence of obesity, poor food choices, and diabetes, a disease linked to diet and exercise. It appeared that our students were consuming too much fat, sugar, flour, and salt, with little or no exercise.

Our education system would lean toward teaching students to become a whole, healthy, and more productive person. Outside the classroom, those basics are often forgotten. We sought to bring healthy, balanced diets and regular doctor visits to keep those student brains operating at full capacity. We tapped into special organizations to gain more knowledge about health and mental clarity.

That spring morning of 2014 was commencement day, and I was excited. I noticed, though, that the closer we got to our starting time, things weren't moving according to plan.

"What's the problem?" I asked the young female coordinator.

"The professors aren't quite ready," she whispered.

"You tell them that we will start on time."

Pomp and circumstance filled the air as the class marched in, right on time. Student and faculty speeches dominated and accolades flourished. Degrees were passed out, and the graduating students took pictures with the president. Because of my knee surgery, I had to sit on a stool and pull students close to take a picture. It seemed that every other person, male and female, was overweight, which only increased my concerns. I knew that particular problem would be ongoing, even after my stay was over.

Problems with timeliness, promptness, readiness, and deadlines were endemic to our community. I noted the administration always waited until the last minute to file reports, as if we were not conducting a business. University business is a *business*. Should anyone come up with a project, contract, or last-minute scheme, I refused to sign off. It was my responsibility to put a permanent stop to shabby habits, and I had clearly laid out all principles and details to make that a part of the university archives and active rules to follow long after I was gone.

My job description was to counter some of the negatives that were not in the best interest of Tuskegee's growth and student welfare. I stopped employees from spending their work time on personal business. Since my arrival, I started bringing that loose-ship operation to a well-defined route.

Having finished spring 2014 commencement and being at the end of my tour of duty, a new president was selected. I felt we had made great strides. Most of the people on the faculty and staff at Tuskegee understood why we needed to change the culture of the university, and that understanding would be the only way changes would continue long after my wife and I returned home.

In order to protect the policies and habits we had implemented, I wanted to embed them into the tapestry of that fine university. I wrote them to become policy, a blueprint to guide them back to wholeness. Here are most of the items I put in print:

* University property is not yours to give away.
* Customer service is the university's best asset.
* The university is to aid staff in serving the public and students, not the other way around.
* University is established to be a service provider.
* When people visit the campus, show an active interest in them.
* When the university is obligated to pay somebody at a certain time, appropriate personnel will be made aware of it, and the institution will take action.
* The university is no longer allowed to make commitments that it cannot keep.
* When the phone rings, an assigned staff member will answer promptly in a friendly and professional manner.
* If the professional in charge does not have answers for visitors, he or she will find appropriate answers.
* The assigned staff member will promptly return the call with the answer.

This was the kind of system my administration left with staff, faculty, and students at Tuskegee in June 2014.

The Tuskegee University community, as a whole, had started to buy into this new culture, knowing that they were a part of making the new policy successful.

We were all there for Mother Tuskegee.

Positive possibilities were put to work. The proof of our efforts showed clearly. Two student recruiters were assigned to bring in potential students the following week. When they came, I welcomed the visitors in person. At other times, I went out of my office to talk to visitors. During the recruiting phase, I invited twenty-seven students into my office. Those were practices I added to our policies and procedures, which gave us checks and balances that had not been in place when I arrived.

After I returned home, a board member wrote me a touching letter:

"It was kind of difficult for you at first, but you seemed to have turned this ship around. With a new president coming in, if he can keep it going in the same direction you've set for us, then everything will be all right."

I felt that way too. My wife and I made a great sacrifice to Tuskegee University because we were, and are, passionate about the task we accepted. It means a lot to us, to our family, to black people, and I believe to people in general. It makes a difference to America.

Our efforts proved to be valuable when the largest employer in Mississippi came up to visit Tuskegee. Quite unexpectedly, he saw one of our students walking past us with his shoulders rolled back and his head held high. He was dressed in a neat blue plaid sport shirt and shined shoes. When the employer saw that young man, he touched my arm to interrupt our conversation.

"Young man, what's your name?" he called out.

The young man slowed and nodded. "John Freeman, sir."

"Step over here a minute," the man beckoned.

The young man approached the veranda.

"What are you doing this summer?" the man asked.

"Looking for a job, sir," he said, smiling.

"Well, you look like you are going someplace in life."

"Thank you, sir," the young man said.

"How'd you like to work for me in Mississippi?" The employer reached in his valise and handed him an application form and beckoned him to sit at the table behind us.

The young man sat at the table while the man and I continued our conversation. In the shortest time, he handed the application back to his potential employer who looked over it.

"Okay, you got the job. Now if you do a good job, I'll hire you every summer." He paused. "And when you finish school, we'll hire you with the promise of six month raises."

Even I was stunned. It happened so fast. That moment was the manifestation of what I had been teaching since I arrived at Tuskegee.

"When you step out of your house, dorm, or bedroom in the morning, act as if you were walking onto a stage. Show the audience your attitude, your smile, and your persona. 'I am somebody, I want to be somebody, and I'm going places.'"

That moment was an example of the kind of students we were committed to graduating from Tuskegee University.

CHAPTER 31

❖❖❖

Reflections of a Lifetime
on a Plane Ride Home

Delta Airlines flight 1837 took off smoothly from Atlanta Airport. The first-class ride was comfortable, as was my inner peace. I had planted something good and lasting, something that would reach into the future. A sense of contentment filled my heart the moment Roberta sat in the window seat beside me.

"What are you thinking, Matt?" Roberta asked.

"Everything and nothing." I smiled. She fastened her seat belt and closed her eyes, leaving me with my private thoughts.

I ignored the stewardess's relentless offers of wine, champagne, and liquor. I didn't need a warm towel for my hands or a cool towel for my face. I didn't have time for such trivialities. I was considering the sum total of my eighty years of life.

Who beyond my father and mother shaped my life, my accomplishments, my strength? Where did such a raw desire to add something of value to my people, my family, my country, and this world come from? *Was it some planetary essence in my personality that shined an intuitive light?*

By that time, the plane was cruising at thirty thousand feet, and the stars outside shined distant and mysterious. I leaned back and allowed my thoughts to carry me back to the farm.

I was home on a holiday break from Tuskegee, driving down County Road 64 in Alabama. My headlights pierced the pitch black before me. I rumbled along, heading home, feeling the calm of nightfall.

Suddenly, I was blinded by a bright light and felt a violent impact. I was being crushed as screaming metal filled my consciousness.

I was thrown across the passenger's seat, avoiding certain death.

It happened so quickly. One moment, I was calmly driving home by the light of my own headlights; the next moment, I was staring into a brighter light and crushed, unsure if I was dead or alive.

A man sitting in the pulpwood truck in the middle of the road sustained a broken neck and died instantly. The pulpwood truck had a metal bar that stretched across the back section. It could have cut me in half under ordinary circumstances, except luck was on my side.

Back then, southern men would often park their cars and trucks in the middle of country roads and drink booze. I never knew if the other man was drinking, but why on earth was he in the middle of the road if he wasn't nipping?

That question would ride heavy on my conscience for a lifetime.

In 2012, more than sixty years after that accident, my brother Samuel and I were driving down County Road 64. We approached an intersection with a flashing red stoplight. Samuel stopped at the intersection, and *wham!* A car slammed into our side. The force flipped the car over with us inside.

It took me a second to realize what had happened. We had been driving to Samuel's house, enjoying our conversation on a sunny fall afternoon when a loud noise thrust us to the ceiling of the car. I could see blood dripping down as we hung upside down, held in place by our seatbelts. I knew I was alive when I heard my own voice.

"You all right?" I asked Samuel.

"My neck hurts."

"Car hit us," I said.

Wearing seat belts had just saved our lives. Paramedics and police arrived some time later. They pried open my door and pulled me out. To my surprise, I was unharmed except for a split lip from the airbag. I stood there watching as they moved to the driver's side, hoping Samuel was okay. We were hit on his side of the car that was now smashed flat. The rescue team used the jaws of life to free Samuel of the wreckage. He was unharmed.

That accident was a testament to modern automotive engineering. The car was demolished, but we were unharmed. Logically, I knew why we had survived, but it felt like a miracle, nonetheless. I felt the blessing of life.

We were blessed because we never saw the car coming. That position kept us calm. *A body at rest tends to stay at rest.* Had we known it was coming, our muscles would have tensed up, and we probably would have sustained serious injury. The larger blessing was that I survived an accident on the same road where a man died, where I nearly died, as a college student. I had, once more, been given the gift of life.

Since then, I have had successes, setbacks, heartbreaks, and goals to fulfill. As an older man, walking away from another wreck on County Road 64, I realize that life amounts to one thing: always believe in *positive possibilities.*

No matter how bleak life may get, if you are alive, you have an opportunity to do something positive. The gift of life means knowing there are unseen possibilities. It means having more time to manifest dreams into goals, make new game plans, and bring about hard-earned realities. The greatest humans in history have all responded to adversity with courage and the understanding that *positive possibilities* are there, unseen, for you to accept or reject.

I suggest that you accept them in every critical situation of your life.

Like a bright light in the darkest night, I'm going to keep going until I stop. Every day my eyes open, I'll take in the light of day with vigor, seeking out the *positive possibilities* around me. I drive Roberta crazy the way I push myself. My physical body doesn't always let me do all that I desire, but I push back. I still rise early in the morning, exercise, and read three or four newspapers before most people wake up. Sometimes, my back or my knees act up, but I don't let that get me down. I focus on *positive possibilities* to make the best of my lot in life.

Recently, I had a talk with my son Dexter about challenges he was facing. Several years ago, Dexter developed multiple sclerosis. This came as a shock to the entire family. Suddenly, Dexter—who was always healthy, who excelled in school, and who was poised for a promising professional career—faced a chronic disease that would change the course of his life.

Over the years, I have been extremely proud of the way Dexter quietly persevered through the many physiological and neurological assaults that MS brought upon him. But all of us have our limits, and there came a day not too long ago when it seemed to me that MS was getting the best of him. Dexter was hurting so much that he was not able to project his usual positive attitude to his wife and children.

I understood how hard it was for Dexter to deal with his new reality. Life had thrown him a nasty curveball. So one day, I sat with Dexter, and we talked. I told him I understood the grief and frustration he faced. I empathized with him because he's my flesh and blood; his hopes and despairs are mine. It pains me immensely that he has MS.

Life is not always fair, but it is always a gift.

"You could have died," I told Dexter.

He nodded.

I felt hopeful that he was still alive. Life can be brutal, but it should also be joyous. Dexter is blessed with a beautiful family that loves him. He can still gaze into the bright, hopeful eyes of his children. He can share his example of how to persevere in the face of adversity. Reaching beyond ourselves to help others, even when it hurts, is the essence of pursuing a higher calling. That is my hope for members of my family and every family.

CHAPTER 32

※⟨8⟩※

Knowing Hurt and Rejection and Erasing Corruption

Inside the soft roar of the plane and the sight of a stewardess offering champagne, I see a man's face that I have not thought about in a long time. But my heart does not flutter with anger. It beats with the easy rhythm of forgiveness. If I could give him one thing, it would be to show him how much corruption he spreads into society. I would give him that information with kindness.

You see, my dad's disadvantages prepared me for a progressive future. He watched and learned how plantation owners reasoned and negotiated business dealings. He used that know-how to build an award-winning farming industry. The family passed that know-how and the responsibility on to me. Having been instilled with the story of my father's history served me well when the board chairman ignored me while introducing every other board member to the visitors who came to pay their respects. I asserted myself and greeted the visitors without his introduction because I refused to be invisible.

In Ralph Ellison's *Invisible Man*, his character, similar to mine in that board member situation, came out of the basement and joined society again because he no longer hated. He no longer needed to be seen as anything but who he was. He now tolerated people who could not see him.

I am fortunate to own the gift of grace in the face of discrimination. Grace requires me to believe that I am no better than anyone else and nobody else is any better than me.

A static-laden weather report played in the cabin, but I was wrapped in the recall of the third phase of my life, and I wouldn't allow anything to interfere.

So what's left for me to do on earth?

I open my eyes to invisible injustice, which includes remnants of the white entitlement complex that skews the thinking of too many people. Modern science can no longer use the old totem-pole concepts of race, where the whitest-skinned figures are on top and the racial castes and colors are below, indicating a rank of superiority or inferiority in terms of whiteness. That notion is not only false to me but also utter foolishness. That notion of race is wickedly divisive in ways that go far beyond black and white distinctions. There is greatness, super intelligence, bigotry, and ignorance in every gradation of skin tone.

Over the years, I've heard people of Mediterranean or Middle Eastern descent become indignant or angry if they are perceived to be Mexican or Central or South American. I've seen people with very dark skin describe themselves as white. All such nonsense is the wrong focus. These silly totem-pole notions of racial superiority must be eliminated and replaced with an egalitarian vision, where all humans stand on the same ground, treating each other as equals. Man can no longer exploit self-importance, richness, and superiority on the backs of other humans. Human beings, especially those that represent a democratic society, cannot discriminate based upon superstition and bogus concepts of race—egalitarianism!

——◆◆◆——

I hear the laughter of my best friend.

As the plane shakes while coming through a patch of clouds, I smile at the friends, enemies, and times that have made me who I am. My best friend Dick Fink had a name that, at first utterance, made him sound like a contemptible villain in a hard-boiled crime novel. To the contrary, Dick was one of the most admirable people I've ever met.

Dick Fink, a short white man, was my best friend. He subscribed to *Anthem*, *Ebony*, and *JET* magazines because he wanted to make sure his kids, who were white, had exposure to cultures other than their own. He knew the world would be increasingly ethnic and more culturally diverse in the future, and he wanted his kids to realize the kind of world they would be living in.

For years, my family and Dick's family, along with another white family and a Japanese-Chinese family, traveled all over the world together. As our children grew and our careers evolved, Dick and I remained the best of friends. We both believed in justice, equality, and having fun! We went on ski trips, we golfed, and Dick was there for both my holes in one. We played golf twice a week.

We shared many laughs at social gatherings. On one occasion, at a swanky party in Hollywood, I was having a friendly dance with Zsa Zsa Gabor. Dick broke in and asked, "Would you mind dancing with a short little white man?"

I first met Dick when he contacted me to support the rabies prevention program that he was pushing as president of the Southern California Veterinary Medical Association. I signed on and Dick, and I quickly became great friends and allies.

We used to talk about problems linked to racism, and we both agreed that it all came back to the golden rule: treat everybody the way you want to be treated, irrespective of ethnicity, gender, or religion. Dick eventually became president of the American Veterinary Medical Association (AVMA), and he took his positive values to the heights of our profession. He was a sterling example of a leader whose values were the same for his family, his community, and his business. He and I could not have been closer friends. Philosophically and morally, we were on the same page.

He was born on a farm in Illinois, so both of us could relate to the values of our agrarian upbringing.

Sometimes, Dick would say, "Matt, you ought to hear some of the things those white boys say when you're not around." Dick was not one to go along to get along. "They won't say it when you're around, but when we're alone, they're prejudiced. So I tell them they're full of shit."

Dick didn't stop with tough talk; he walked the walk and paved the way to get me on the agenda at that AVMA convention in Las Vegas in July 1970. During one of my speeches at that convention, I said, "Ladies and gentlemen, as you look around the room, I want you to ask yourselves why it is that I am the only black person in this room. Why is that?"

I paused.

"General Snider can tell you. If you were to go to Vietnam right now, you would find a whole lot of black soldiers. They're defending our rights. They're defending the right for you to come here and have this meeting. And a lot of them are going to die for this country. They're going to die for each and every person in this room."

There was not a sound.

"Blacks just want to participate in every aspect of American society, be it veterinary medicine, farming, politics, and sometimes even war. Members of the AVMA, deans of veterinary schools, presidents of colleges, and many veterinarians are concerned about the small number of minority veterinarians in this country. An insufficient number of minorities apply to veterinary schools and fewer still are admitted. Other professional associations have recognized this lack of diversity and addressed the issue by establishing recruitment programs. I strongly urge you, distinguished members of the AVMA, to do the same."

I remembered that indistinguishable commentary swirling in the background.

"Something's wrong when you have two hundred or three hundred people in a room representing the hierarchy of veterinary medicine in this country and there is not one black face in attendance. I think that indicates that the AVMA needs to recruit black representation to be among its house of delegates and executive board, as well as the national office."

I concluded my speech with a call to action.

"I would like to see this body rise to the occasion of democracy, not next year, not tomorrow, but today. If we believe in the golden rule, then we should pass my suggested reforms."

That day, the proverbial arc of the moral universe bent towards equality. The AVMA adopted a new policy that called for the dismissal of any state organization member that practiced discrimination. The reforms also endorsed future plans to address the financial needs to veterinary schools, which included Tuskegee Institute. It also voiced support for the value of placing blacks in positions of authority throughout the AVMA.

We adopted legislation that day which outlawed discrimination in the American Veterinary Medicine Association. I am particularly thankful that I had such a close friend and ally as Dick Fink to advocate on behalf of those reforms. Dick could have very easily positioned himself in the Good Old Boys Club and done nothing to help minority veterinarians, but he knew better. He knew that people in America and around the world comprise a wide range of cultural, religious, and ethnic backgrounds, and each should be respected. He also knew that there is only one human race.

All my golfing buddies are dead now. My friend Ralph Vierheller hit a long drive and fell dead. Dick Fink was sitting at his kitchen table one day and asked his daughter to go get him an aspirin. When she returned, he was dead. Bob Whitford went for a walk, and when he returned home, he fell dead right in his own doorway.

I am the last man standing. And I stand before you now, before the world, to honor their integrity and humanity that makes our world a better place to live.

—◄·❈·►—

The plane ride was so smooth that I fell into a dreamlike walk with my dear friend, Dr. Frederick Patterson.

I miss walking with Dr. Frederick Patterson. I miss talking sports and politics with Dr. Dick Fink. And I miss catching shows or grabbing a bite to eat with Dr. Mark Sternfeld.

I recall how Dr. Sternfeld continued to pester me about coming back to New York and taking over the practice, my answer was always the same, "I'm going to California."

Unlike most white practitioners, Dr. Sternfeld took a chance on getting an intern from Tuskegee. Although everyone in the class applied, he chose me. Arriving at his office in Mt. Vernon, NY, at 7pm, with the office full and many standing outside in line, I grabbed a smock and we didn't finish until 10pm. He seemed to treat me like a son he wished he had. We would go down to New York City and catch the Rockettes, Broadway shows and have dinner in fancy restaurants. In the past, his interns had always come from Cornell University but after me, he switched his allegiance and preference to Tuskegeeans.

Those exemplary human beings were veterinarians and ardent defenders of the golden rule. It didn't matter that we were black, Jewish, or white. All that mattered was that we shared humane and wholesome values, that we each intrinsically understood that we were all part of the same tribe.

In the spring of 2013, I visited Tuskegee to attend the Tuskegee Veterinary Symposium. During the event, I met the president-elect of the AVMA, Dr. Ted Cohn, a man who embodied the values I shared with Patterson, Sternfeld, and Fink. Ted told me that, even when he was a young boy in Little Rock, Arkansas, he had known he wanted to become a veterinarian. He recalled telling his mother that, after reading about Dr. George Washington Carver, he wanted to study veterinary medicine at the Tuskegee Institute. His mother told him that it would not be possible for him to attend a historically black university because he was white. Ted could not understand why it mattered that he was white and other students at Tuskegee were black.

Ted intuitively understood what many adults during that era would never grasp: racial concepts that unite people. Historically, black colleges and universities (HBCUs) like Tuskegee University were established to give African Americans access to higher education they would have not have otherwise received. But as opportunities for black students gradually improved, HBCUs have also made strides in promoting diversity within their ranks.

As Ted and I continued our conversation, I was delighted to learn that, by the time he was college aged, he could attend Tuskegee University's veterinary school, after all.

I find it ironic that for many years the AVMA would not accept students from a historical black school into its association, and now as a white Tuskegee grad, he had become the head of the National Organization of Veterinary Medicine.

⬥⬥⬥

Like it or not, every human must deal with tragedy. Loved ones will get sick and die, and other unexpected misfortunes and calamities will occur. Such events cause emotional and physical pain, and my family has been no different.

Roberta and I had a little girl named Tanya, who was born with microcephaly, a debilitating disease that crushed her tiny life and our hearts in the process. Seeing your own child dying in a hospital bed is an excruciating experience. It leaves you feeling utterly helpless. While little Tanya struggled, we devoted all our energies to her needs. Life seemed to stop. Tragedy has a way of paralyzing one with grief.

When it became clear to Roberta and me that Tanya was going to leave us, we talked about how to proceed. We decided the best way to heal from Tanya's loss was to reach out to another child. We contacted an adoption agency and learned that a baby boy needed a home. We brought our adopted son home on Tuesday, and our daughter Tanya passed away on Friday.

Giving to others when you are hurting is the best way to heal; turning inward will only magnify your grief. It is, of course, very important to take time to grieve. No one should ever rush the healing process or be afraid to ask for help.

There is no shame in recognizing pain and attempting to heal. Repression is dangerous, and it can boil up like a volcano and manifest itself years later if it's not dealt with up front. Recovering from tragedy requires proactive thoughts and action. It's not easy, but it will help you put the pieces of a normal life back together. Helping others when you're hurting is the best way to heal.

All we can do is be good to each other and live the best lives that we can.

CHAPTER 33

<figure>❦</figure>

Who Am I When a Killer Is in My Hospital?

I felt only the slightest movement of the plane, but it didn't disturb me. My mind returned to the most horrible event of my veterinary practice. Around eight o'clock on that fateful night, I received a call from the police.

"Is this Dr. Jenkins?"

"Yes," I answered.

"There's been a murder at your hospital."

"What?" I asked, stunned.

"The female working the night shift has been murdered at your animal hospital."

His words devastated me to my core. Even now, decades later, it deeply pains me to think of that poor young woman in a struggle for her life. She was serving what was to have been her final shift before returning to Alabama to begin her next semester in college.

I had to call that girl's mother in Alabama, the hardest call I've ever had to make. I was hurting almost beyond my capacity to breathe, but I knew this mother's pain would be far beyond my own. For years afterward, I called that mother to check in and let her know I was thinking about her. When tragedy strikes, sometimes, there is nothing you can do except console those who are suffering. That's how I felt then.

It wasn't usual for me to allow women to work night shifts because I was a bit concerned about their safety. But then, the state of California instituted new laws that defined that practice as discriminatory, so I had to let women work the night shift if they applied. My intern requested and applied, and I hired her.

About a year after her murder, I received another call from the police. It was eerily similar to the previous call, like horrible déjà vu.

"Is this Dr. Jenkins?"

"Yes."

"We're holding your supervisor," the policeman said. "He raped your night attendant."

When I told Roberta about the rape, it struck me that the supervisor must have committed the murder a year before. Suddenly, it all made sense. I had observed this supervisor dropping by the hospital during times he was not assigned to work.

"What are you doing here?" I asked one night.

"Just checking to see if everything's okay," he said.

As he was a deacon at a local church and a competent worker, I didn't think much about it. But this time, as he was raping the female night attendant, the telephone rang. He turned her loose to answer the call. It was her boyfriend. Fortunately, the boyfriend could hear distress in her voice and thought to ask the right questions.

"Are you in trouble?" he asked.

"Yes," she said.

"Do you want me to call the police?"

"Yes," she said.

Within five minutes, the doorbell rang.

The supervisor let her go to answer the door. Police charged in and freed the young woman from her tormentor. The following day, the supervisor called me and asked me to be a witness in his defense.

"You don't want me for your defense," I said.

He blew up and threatened me, but I didn't sweat it because I knew he would be in jail for a very long time.

—◆◃✦▹◆—

I have worked with quite a few university presidents over the years; some were eagles, and some were turkeys. In this regard, John Maguire unquestionably belongs in the eagle flock. John was a close friend and collaborator with Martin Luther King, Jr., a freedom rider and fierce advocate for liberty and justice. I have noticed that all the people I respect the most have stood up for egalitarianism and the golden rule.

After King's assassination in Memphis, John traveled to the King residence in Atlanta the night before the funeral. He arrived sometime after 11:00 p.m. Many people had visited, and the house was in disarray. John asked Coretta Scott King's associate, Bernita Bennett, what he could do to help. Bernita handed him a broom and said, "You can sweep."

John took the broom without hesitation and swept the floors as the midnight hour passed. Coretta visited John for a time as he swept, and they exchanged heartfelt words. She maintained that anyone could be great if they serve. I believe John exemplified that notion of service when he swept the King residence on that sad day in 1968.

<hr />

A rough patch of air in the landing path took me to the arena of Peaceful Solutions by asking questions.

It takes real discipline to stay silent when you're angry. There's a lot of cultural chatter about being cool, but that's superficial. What I'm talking about is the ability to reject the impulse to release your anger. If you can keep a cool head when you're feeling hot, that's a skill to be admired, and it's a skill that can be learned.

Getting angry is a choice, but if you train yourself to resist those impulses, life becomes much easier to navigate. Resisting fits of anger can be difficult, especially when others around you are angry. You hold it and you hold it and you hold it, and the more you hold it, the more the other person decompresses. I have faced situations so intense that I forced myself to write down these words:

Stay cool. Refrain from making statements, as this can antagonize. The far more fruitful approach is to ask questions.

You see, when you ask a question, you are asking the person what he thinks. Questions can unlock new *positive possibilities* in your mind and the minds of others.

Even if you're dealing with unreasonable people, really screwed-up people, you'll get nowhere by saying how screwed up they are. But a well-positioned question can be a game changer. Only the cool headed are able to use calm and reasonable observation and inquiry to bring about *positive possibilities*.

The actual experience I refer to happened long ago, back when I owned my first mobile home park. That day, I came to remove one of my managers after several warnings about his substandard managerial performance. When I arrived, he was sitting in the living room near a window, picking on a guitar, all tattooed up. Word had gotten to me that he was a gang member.

"I came by to tell you I'm no longer going to need your services."

He slammed down the guitar. "Faggot! You come here to tell me that?"

I didn't say a word. I just looked at him calmly. Finally, after calling me every name in the book, his wife came into the room.

"Jeff, I am so disappointed in you!" she said and then looked toward me. "Dr. Jenkins, you should have fired us a long time ago."

Her husband stomped around for a few seconds while I remained silent. When he finally cooled down, I asked, "When can you be out?"

"Two o'clock," he answered.

"Okay," I said and walked outside.

I tell this story to reinforce my belief that the practice of listening and keeping a cool head helped turn a volatile situation into a peaceful solution. I have found this approach to be useful with all kinds of people, but most importantly, my wife.

—◄·❈·►—

The strategy of listening and asking questions holds true. I recall another occasion that was even more volatile than the mobile home park incident. It was a moment when listening and asking questions probably saved my life.

It was long ago, at the beginning of my real-estate acquisitions, when I went to collect rent on a small house we owned in Compton. I walked inside the small living room and asked the renter for the $240 he owed.

"I'll get it to you," he said.

"You told me that the last four times I was here," I said.

"You can't get blood outta a turnip." He went to the kitchen table and then whirled around holding a switchblade. His eyes were filled with rage. I stood my ground as calmly as I could and didn't say a word. *Stay cool, set my game plan quickly, and stay the course.*

With the switchblade in my face, I had one goal: to get out of that house alive and unharmed.

I kept looking into his eyes in a very calm manner so as not to incite his anger, as I steadied my stance so in case he lunged at me, I could grab his arm and deflect the blow. I breathed slowly and steadily, never glancing away from him.

After what seemed like hours, he calmed down and laid the knife back on the table. I hadn't said a single word. My core set of practices and values had worked, and I knew that they would work in the future.

I purposely avoided combat with the man, as I knew that was the key to getting him to calm down, to put him at ease rather than confront him. I had learned that people who become enraged don't respond to talk and accusations. That was the power of actively listening: paying attention to the responses and the emotional state of the person in crisis.

It had been unnerving to stand there and stare into the eyes of a man who was waving a sharp blade between us. I had to constantly remind myself to focus on reflecting kindness and patience. After he put the knife away, I asked, "How much time will you need?"

"Tonight," he said.

I walked out of that house unscathed and climbed into my old VW, thankful that I was alive.

Looking back, it seemed that the switchblade incident embodied the practices and values that began to inspire this book long before people started telling me to write it. How to succeed when confronted with life's inevitable challenges, most of which involved some vital social component.

CHAPTER 34

Times Are a Changing

"We're an hour outside of Los Angeles. Soon, you'll be asked to put your trays in the upright position and—"

The captain's voice was only a slight intrusion into my recollections. It had been three hours, and it seemed as if it were only minutes. I turned my head to the right and went back to my dreamy contemplation.

It's been over sixty years since the supreme court handed down its landmark decision in Brown versus Board of Education. Surely, we have progressed from those ugly scenes of African American students being escorted into a school building by military guards because of threats of violence.

Or have we?

It's all too easy to become comfortable thinking about the advances we have made and to ignore current challenges in equality and the advances we still need to make.

Social progress is like swimming. If you are content with treading water, riptides will pull you farther and farther from the shores of justice. A candid review of American history reveals that legal bodies from the US Supreme Court all the way down to local school boards have been complicit in maintaining white superiority in education. The current supreme court would probably not approve a Civil Rights Bill today.

State governments are passing (or manipulating) laws that make it more difficult for minorities to register to vote. Look at some of the things that Republican officials did to denigrate President Barack Obama.

In many respects, Obama experienced the presidential equivalent of what Jack Johnson and Jackie Robinson experienced when they crossed the color lines in boxing and baseball.

When Rep. Joe Wilson, R-S.C., yelled, "You lie!" in the middle of Obama's speech before Congress in 2009, it was clear that the office had been disrespected. Republicans and Democrats alike immediately criticized Wilson, but it was clear that there was more at play than typical partisanship. I've been a close observer of presidential politics for decades, and I've never seen any senator or representative disrespect a president like Wilson did. There were too many disrespectful and repugnant acts against President Obama to name, but one thing was clear: many of those unfortunate acts are symptoms of racist views.

Fortunately, it just so happens that Obama defied the typical stereotypes attached to black American males. He has a beautiful family, he's loyal to his tremendous wife, he is always informed and composed, and he never resorts to the politics of anger or resentment. He's a class act that blew up all the typical stereotypes. But while I am very impressed by Obama, I also realize that he is just one man. It is up to every American to be vigilant and keep pushing for liberty and justice.

I agree with Van Jones when he said, "For a while at least, many were so enthralled with the idea of being a part of history that we forgot the courage, sacrifices, and risks that are sometimes required to make history."

Obama did, indeed, make history when he became the first president of African American heritage. But that achievement did not signal the end of racism. In fact, it brought out the worst in social acceptance. It dredged up the worst of our past and challenged the best of our aspirations that have spanned centuries to secure liberty and justice for all.

When Obama was first elected, it was a novelty. Everybody felt warm and fuzzy. And then the old guard came in and things became more toxic and partisan in Washington than ever before. What is the solution? It's really about forming independent movements outside the beltway, far from the world of lobbyists and insider politics, to push heads of state to do the right thing.

As president, Franklin Delano Roosevelt did not lead the labor movement. That was the job of independent union leaders. The alchemy of political power and people power resulted in the New Deal. As president, Woodrow Wilson did not lead the fight to enfranchise women. That was the role of independent movement leaders, such as suffragettes Susan B. Anthony and Ida B. Wells. The alchemy of political power and people power resulted in the women's right to vote.

As president, Abraham Lincoln did not lead the abolitionists. That was the job of independent movement leaders like Frederick Douglass, John Brown, and Harriet Tubman. The alchemy of political power and people power resulted in the emancipation of enslaved Africans.

As president, Richard Nixon didn't lead the environmental movement. That was the job of environmental organizations such as the Sierra Club and leaders, like the writer Rachel Carson. Once again, it was the alchemy of political power and people power that resulted in the Clean Air Act, the Clean Water Act, and the Environmental Protection Agency.

If American citizens stand by waiting for politicians to fix their problems, nothing will happen. I want to see people standing up for the things that are right, no matter what they are and no matter what the cost. If something is wrong, don't sit silently. Stand up and be counted. This is a great country. Don't do it a disservice by remaining silent in the presence of bigotry, intolerance, or unfairness.

Roberta and I participated in antidiscrimination rallies with Dr. Martin Luther King, Jr. in Los Angeles. We picketed in Dominguez Hills and Torrance, California, against the practice of African Americans and nonwhites being denied access to new housing subdivisions. Participating in those picket lines reflected our deepest values, and those same values have always inspired us to treat our employees like family.

We follow the golden rule in all our dealings. We believe that no human being is better than any other human being.

"Injustice anywhere is a threat to justice everywhere," as Martin Luther King, Jr. wrote in *Letter from a Birmingham Jail*.

I wholeheartedly concur with his belief that all humans "are caught in an inescapable network of mutuality, tied in a single garment of destiny. Whatever affects one directly, affects all indirectly."

Those who have championed this belief, such as Harry Belafonte and many other upholders of truth, understood that every member of the human race is from the same tribe.

I have great hope for humanity, for America, and for our youth.

I will keep working for the things I believe in for as long as I draw breath, with Roberta at my side.

"Please fasten your seat belts and get ready to land in Los Angeles," the stewardess announced.

We had been in the air for four hours and were now descending to the Los Angeles airport, nearly home with our contribution to Tuskegee and Tuskegee's gift of allowing my wife and me to impact the lives of so many young people. I felt complete. My experience at Tuskegee will always remain a part of my fondest memories forever.

WHAT WILL MATTER?

Ready or not, someday, it will all come to an end. There will be no more sunrises, no minutes, hours, or days. All things you collected, whether treasured or forgotten, will pass to someone else.

Your wealth, fame, and temporal power will shrivel to irrelevance. Your grudges, resentments, frustrations, and jealousies will finally disappear. So too your hopes, ambitions, plans, and to-do lists will expire.

The wins and losses that once seemed so important will fade away. It won't matter where you came from or on what side of the tracks you lived at the end.

It won't matter whether you were beautiful or brilliant. Even your gender and skin color will be irrelevant.

So what will matter? How will the value of your days be measured?

What will matter is not what you bought, but what you built; not what you got, but how you gave.

What will matter is not your success, but your significance. What will matter is not what you learned, but what you taught.

What will matter is every act of integrity, compassion, courage, or sacrifice that enriched, empowered, or encouraged others to emulate your example.

What will matter is not your competence, but your character. What will matter is not how many people you knew, but how many will feel a lasting loss when you're gone.

What will matter are not your memories, but the memories that live in those who loved you.

What will matter is how long you will be remembered, by whom, and for what.

Living a life that matters doesn't happen by accident. It's not a matter of circumstance but of choice.

Choose to live a life that matters.

—Michael Josephson

ABOUT THE AUTHOR

Matthew Jenkins grew up in Southern Alabama, one of ten children. He graduated from Tuskegee University with a degree in veterinary medicine. Matthew served in the United States Air Force. During the time he was stationed in Greenland, he was the first person to discover rabies in that country and later led a team dedicated to the control and eradication of this disease. After his military service, Matthew entered into private practice in Compton, California. Dr. Jenkins developed a new anesthetic combination for cats, and the results were published in Modern Veterinary Practice, February 1972 edition. This drug is now used in many countries around the world.

In 1970, Matthew appeared before the National American Veterinary Medical Association and was responsible for resolutions, which resulted in the dismissal of any state that practiced discrimination against minority veterinarians by excluding them from membership in the American Veterinary Medical Association (AVMA). He also introduced resolutions, which resulted in placing African Americans in positions of authority within the AVMA, including the establishment of a program for the recruitment of minority students.

Matthew and his wife Roberta founded Saroe Imports in 1970 and in 1974 and created SDD Enterprises, Inc., a highly successful real-estate investment and property management firm with businesses in eight states.

In addition to his veterinary degree, Matthew was honored by his alma mater with an honorary doctor of science. He has served on the boards of numerous educational institutions and community and business organizations while being recognized for his leadership, inspiration, and example.

Matthew served as the interim president of Tuskegee University during the 2013–2014 school year.

Matthew and his wife Roberta founded the Matthew and Roberta Jenkins Family Foundation in 1984. The foundation has been responsible for providing numerous scholarships across the country to many deserving students, colleges, and institutions.

Positive Possibilities: My Game Plan for Success, which describes the challenges Matthew and his wife faced in the journey of reaching the pinnacles of their careers, is Matthew Jenkins's first published book.

Matthew is married to fellow Tuskegee graduate Roberta Jones Jenkins. They are the proud parents of three children—Sabrae, Derryl and Dexter and six grandchildren - Makarios, Zowey, Olivia, Bianca, Dominic and Amaris.